Publishing
Your Family History
on the Internet

Publishing
Your Family History
on the Internet

By Richard S. Wilson

First Edition, 1999

Published by:
Compuology
330 La Serna Drive
La Habra, CA 90631-2801
Phone: (562) 690-5588
E-mail: sales@compuology.com

Distributed to the trade by Betterway Books
an imprint of F & W Publications, Inc.
1507 Dana Avenue
Cincinnati, OH 45207
1-800/289-0963

First printing, March, 1999
10 9 8 7 6 5 4 3 2

Printed in the United States of America.

ISBN 0-938717-36-7

Library of Congress Catalog Card Number: 97-80735

About the Author

Richard S. Wilson

Richard S. Wilson brings more than fourteen years of online experience to this publication and has been doing genealogical research for more than nineteen years. He is a nationally known genealogical and computing lecturer, has written articles for international magazines, and is a contributing editor to the *NGS/CIG Digest*. He is the owner of Compuology (**http://www.compuology.com/**) a genealogical-based computer company. He received his Bachelors Degree from the California State University, Long Beach and has taught a monthly Computer Interest Group (CIG) for the Whittier Area Genealogy Society (WAGS) from 1992 to 1997.

Richard is currently the state coordinator for the California USGenWeb Project on the Internet, the president of the Southern California Chapter Association of Professional Genealogists and the secretary of the Genealogical Speakers Guild. He is co-author of *The Internet for Genealogists: A Beginner's Guide*. His genealogical memberships include the Genealogical Speakers Guild, the National Genealogical Society (NGS), the Association of Professional Genealogists (APG), the California State Genealogical Alliance, a life membership in the Whittier Area Genealogy Society, as well as many other local genealogical and historical societies. He can be reached through at his e-mail address of *<wilson@compuology.com>* or *<richardw@earthlink.net>*.

Acknowledgments

There are many people who have assisted me in getting this book completed and in its final form. I would first like to thank my wife, Carol, for all of her reinforcement and encouragement. I would also like to thank the many creators of the Internet who made it such a wonderful place to bring together researchers and the increasing amounts of data and digitized original sources for which they search.

I would especially like to thank Barbara Renick for all her contributions and encouragements. Without her help this book would not have been possible. She always gives her assistance in a very unselfish way.

And of course I would like to thank all of the others who have assisted with proofreading and reformatting the initial drafts of this book. There are many who have contributed their thoughts and ideas to make this book what it is today.

I would like to thank Cyndi Howells for the encouragement and support she has given me. I would also like to thank Ken McGinnis and Dave Berdan, with Millennia Corporation, for all the additional efforts they put into adding Web page creation to their Legacy program. Also Gary B. Shumway, with Advanced Digital for his help with the cover and layout of this book.

Foreword

Do not waste your time searching the Internet—let others do the work for you—let them locate your genealogy site. This book was developed to help the genealogist discover how easy and beneficial it is to publish their family history on the Internet. It is easy to convert genealogical data into Web pages. This book will help you design and create those pages, discover ways to get Web space and advertizing for free, and how to install your Web site on the Internet.

Publishing Your Family History on the Internet is also very beneficial for genealogists with more experience on the Web. It discusses ideas, topics and links to Web sites that are of interest to genealogists with varying experience levels on the Web.

The operations of many programs are covered in this book. Normally they are listed in alphabetical order, not in an order of preference. No one program will be recommended and probably no one program will have all the features you are looking for.

While reading this book, if you encounter terms or acronyms you do not understand, turn to the Glossary. A lot of work went into the Glossary to make it as complete as possible. It will also help you understand computers and the Internet in general.

Symbols Used in this Book

 Helpful Hints

 Richard's Comments

 Technical Note

 Warning

 Be aware that to successfully publish your genealogy on the Internet you may have to learn to use several different types of software and learn a new vocabulary too. The actual effort, once you learn how to create genealogy Web pages, takes only minutes and the rewards are great. So grit your teeth, dig in here, and you will reap a world of benefits for your efforts.

Table of Contents

Table of Illustrations

Why Publish
Your Family History
on the Web?

Chapter 1

Exposure

Have you ever submitted a query to a genealogical publication, periodical, or newsletter? Most genealogists have discovered that queries bring great benefits. Everyone has heard stories about people finding information on a missing ancestor from a query they posted. Well, imagine being able to submit your genealogical query, or data, to a place where it can be read and viewed by hundreds of thousands of genealogists all over the world—for very little cost. If you are interested in extending any of your family lines back in time, then continue reading.

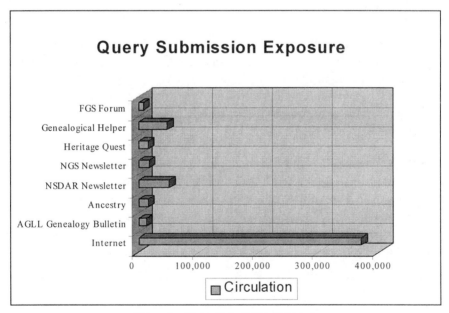

Figure 1: Query Submission Exposure

As you can see in Figure 1, there is no better way to reach so many people around the world. Even the National Society Daughters of the American Revolution (NSDAR) magazine, with their circulation of 50,000 is no match for the 370,000 (and growing) genealogists currently using the Internet. (The data in Figure 1 is from February 1998 statistics, taken from each publisher's circulation data. The Internet statistic is based on the number of users posting queries to the Roots-L mail list.)

Once I created a Web site with some of my family history on it, I was amazed at the response I received. I have found many cousins that I wasn't even aware of. Quite a few of my family lines have been extended back many generations because of contacts from people who have found my family's data on the Internet.

I have received numerous family group sheets, pedigrees, family stories, source documentation, and photographs from other researchers who have located my genealogy on the Web. So far, I have only put a small part of my genealogy on the Internet, so the number of responses I have received is small compared to the results I would get if all of my information was on the Web.

With my genealogical data on the Internet, I also have the added benefit of being able to update and change my data as often as I like, for no additional cost (other than the time involved). You can't do that with genealogical queries or family history books published on paper.

You can view my Web pages at **http://www.compuology.com/richard/**.

If you do not believe there are many genealogists on the Internet who will respond to you and be willing to share their data with you, just read this story told by Kirk Larsen.

> "I've been conducting genealogical research for many years. During this time, I have sent out a couple hundred inquiries via the postal service. I received only two replies for all my effort. Recently, I subscribed to Roots-L and several other genealogical Internet mailing lists. For every five "postings" I placed on these lists, I received an average of 75-100 replies within 5 days. Some only wanted to know what information I already had. Others had corrections or additional data for me. These people were very generous in sharing their research, including biographical information and vital records data. In some instances, they sent me (via the postal service) copies of their research, including photographs, original documents, family bible(s) and heirlooms."

Personal Satisfaction

Still working on that family history book? Still waiting for those last few family members to get their information sent back to you? Maybe you are waiting until you get a chance to check out every possible source and verify all your data. It seems as if we genealogists are always trying to improve and perfect our data and source citations. Will your book ever be ready to publish in your lifetime? Will anyone carry on your work?

The beauty of publishing your family history on the Internet is that a Web page is not cast in concrete. You can place the genealogical research you have completed on the Internet now, then easily add to it or make corrections as more information becomes available. Web pages can be updated monthly, weekly, or even daily (if you have no other demands on your life).

One of the reasons many people have not published their family's history is because of the high cost of publishing paper-bound books. This high cost also pushes us to wait until the materials are more complete. Web publishing eliminates the huge expense of re-publishing a paper-printed and bound book.

Once you have published your family history information on the World Wide Web, interested genealogists and family members (with access to the Internet) can see your information and give you important feedback, with very little cost to them. This can be invaluable as you complete a book or other research project. You also gain the personal satisfaction of knowing you have some of your family history completed.

Richard
Says:

I have been working on genealogy and family history research since
1978. During this time, I have gathered a lot of materials on my family.
However, there are many family members who just do not take the time
to send me materials or stories.

I have not only received a lot of satisfaction from putting my family's
history on the Web, but it gives the family members a chance to see the
data, which prompts them to send me updated materials that can be
posted on my Web site.

Preservation

Once you place your family history on the Internet, no matter what happens to your home computer (which contains your files and data) your work will be preserved. This is because the Web page data is stored on an Internet server (computer) located somewhere else. Should something happen to your computer, you can still retrieve your data from any location in the world with access to the Internet.

While on the subject of preservation, you need to be aware of the importance of backing up the data on your computer. There are many ways of performing backups, such as floppy disks, tape backups, Zip drives, Jazz Drives, and writeable CD ROMs. No matter which method you use, you should make backups every time you make any major changes to your data. Also, you should make more than one type of backup copy of your data, and store them in more than one location.

Web pages are also a great way to preserve those old family photos and documents that are very valuable (irreplaceable). Once they are saved in digital format and placed on the Internet, you know they are safe from fire, flood, earthquake, or theft. You will always be able to get to them again if something happens to your home because they are stored on a computer somewhere else. You can retrieve them with any computer connected to the Internet.

Extend Your Research Contacts

This is one of the most important reasons for having your data published on the Internet. If you have been on the Internet for very long, you have probably spent many hours searching for common ancestors and those elusive distant cousins.

Once you create your own Web site with your genealogy on it, you can sit back and relax. Hundreds of thousands of genealogists on the Internet will now be searching for, and finding, your family history. You are sure to find a distant cousin or others researching common relatives. Having your family's history on the Internet is a great way to make it possible for those distant cousins, and other researchers, to locate you.

The real beauty of contacting others via the Internet is that the exchange of data can happen very quickly and inexpensively. You can send and receive GEDCOM files of family data in just minutes (not weeks, as is typical of the regular postal service). The exchange of digital images and other information is just as quick. All of this can be accomplished by attaching GEDCOM or graphic files to regular e-mail messages. The only delay in exchanging data is the time it takes for the other person to check their e-mail. If both of you are online at the same time, the transfer is almost instantaneous.

Steps to Publishing Genealogical Data on the Web

This all sounds great, but what exactly do you need to get started?

1. Find space on a Web server, connected to the Internet, to store your Web pages (see "Locating Web Space," in *Chapter 6*, on page 179.

2. Identify what information you want to include on your Web site. (Do not worry, you can easily change it if you later change your mind.)

3. Decide how you want to arrange this information on your Web site.

4. Create your Web pages.

5. Check for errors: proofread, inspect, and validate your Web pages for accuracy while they are still on your computer.

6. Upload (send) your pages to your Web server.

7. Check <u>each</u> page, once posted on the Internet, to make sure you can access each of them.

8. Ask friends with different ISP's and different Web browsers to check each of your pages on the Internet to make sure they can access and read them also.

9. Advertise your new Web site.

10. Reap the rewards.

Easing Into
the Language of
Web Pages

## Chapter 2

HTML: a Simple Computer Language

Most of the Web pages you see on the Internet were created with a relatively simple set of special computer codes. The language of the Internet is HTML (this stands for HyperText Markup Language, but you usually see it referred to as just HTML). The beauty of HTML is that it is NOT a complex programming language.

An HTML Web page consists of a plain text document (the kind you can create in any word processor) with special codes added to indicate what attributes, graphics, and links the Web page should have. This is much like the formatting codes seen (or hidden) in word processing programs. These codes, or tags, instruct the Web browser how to format sections of text, display images, and create hot links (connections) to other Internet documents and files. There is no programming involved at any point in creating your Web pages.

So, HTML is nothing more than a set of simple text codes that Web browsers use to interpret the way the page should be displayed. In fact, any Web browser can interpret HTML codes; however, be aware that there are different standards (versions) of the HTML language used on the Internet. The newer versions of HTML allow you to do much more with design features on your Web page.

The standards for the HTML language were set up by an organization called the World Wide Web Consortium (WC3). This group is made up of representatives from various companies. These standards are designated by the small numbers you see after the HTML letters. The newest version of HTML is 4.0 and it has recently been accepted as the new "standard," although most Web browsers still use HTML 3.2 (with their own enhancements). If you design a Web page to work with HTML 4.0 codes, a browser that only supports HTML 3.2 may not be able to display an HTML 4.0 coded page correctly (due to the differences in the versions of HTML used).

If you need further explanation on HTML codes see the complete HTML 3.2 standards page located at: **http://www.w3.org/TR/REC-html32/**.

Microsoft's Internet Explorer 4.0 and Netscape Navigator 4 (the latest versions of each), both support the HTML 4.0 standard. These programs have also added "extended" (extra) commands that allow you to add even more special effects to your Web pages. The catch is that many of these features are readable only if you use that company's Web browser to view such a Web page. Web pages designed with these extended sets of commands look strange, or even unreadable, when seen through any other Web browser.

Figure 2 shows a Web page as viewed with Netscape Navigator 4.

Figure 3 shows the exact same Web page viewed with Lynx, a text only Web browser. As you can see, there is a very large difference when viewing the Internet pages, depending on the Web browser being used.

Figure 2: Web page displayed with Netscape Web Browser

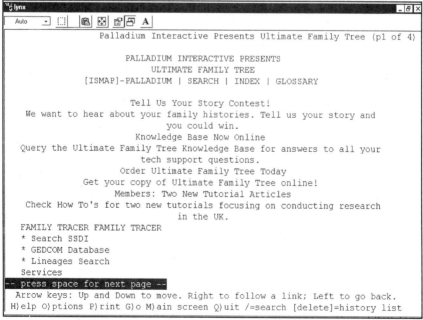

Figure 3: Web page displayed with Lynx (DOS) Web browser

Some Internet Service Providers (hereafter ISPs) use a proprietary browser, such as the one used by Prodigy. If you use one of these proprietary browsers (because of your choice of ISP), you may have problems when you try to display Web pages created with newer HTML standards.

This wide variety of HTML standards and Web browsers leaves you with three choices to make when designing your Web pages:

1. You can stick with the older HTML 3.2 standard and make your pages viewable by most of the people on the World Wide Web. If you choose this option, your Web pages will NOT have the latest and greatest fancy features.

2. You can use the newer HTML 4.0 version and create pages that have advanced design and art features, thus limiting the number of people who can view your pages.

3. You can design two (or more) sets of pages, so that people with different browsers can select which type of page they want to view. If this sounds like twice as much work, it really isn't. It is about as much work as adding a second layer of frosting to a cake. However, you must remember that when you make a change to one set of pages, you must also change the corresponding pages in the other format.

 If you are new to Web page design, I suggest you start learning HTML by designing very simple and basic Web pages (option 1). Then, as you get more comfortable with Web page development, you may want to consider options 2 or 3 above. Remember, it is very easy to change the type and design of your Web pages, once you have created them.

Working With HTML Codes

An HTML document is formatted by enclosing sections of a plain text file between opening and closing tags. Tags are surrounded and identified by less than (<) and greater than (>) symbols, also known as chevrons. (See Figure 4). Most tags come in pairs and are identical, except that the ending tags have a forward slash included in their code, like this: </TAG>.

Tags define how the section of text they enclose will be displayed. Everything after a code such as <B> will be in bold text. Anything after the ending tag </B> will not be in bold text. Tags also create connections to other documents and files, such as multimedia documents (video and sound files). They also cause images to be displayed on your Web pages.

Much of the HTML coding is referred to as "logical markup." Logical markup means that instead of entering each font and its size and spacing, you insert tags which tell the computer how the document is supposed to look. For example, to create the heading at the top of a Web page, tags are inserted around it saying "this is a level one heading" (<H1>), instead of "this piece of text should be displayed in 18 point Times New Roman, bolded, with so much space before it and so much space after it." The details of applying the markup are left up to the browser software used to view the Web page.

It is a good idea to use all caps when typing the HTML codes on the Web pages you create (just the tags, not the file references). Why? Because this causes the tags to stand out from the normal text of the document when you are editing the original plain-text file (just as SURNAMES stand out when we capitalize them). This makes the process of locating errors easier. It is recommended that you follow this HTML coding standard in all of your Web documents.

HTML codes are very basic. The major challenge you will encounter is placing those codes in the proper locations to get the effect you want. Figure 4 shows an example of a very simple Web (HTML) page and following it is an explanation of the codes.

```
<HTML>
<HEAD>
<TITLE> Title of Your Document </TITLE>
</HEAD>
<BODY>
Simple Page
</BODY>
</HTML>
```

Figure 4:   Simple Web page codes

HTML - This indicates that this is an HTML document suitable for viewing or displaying on the World Wide Web portion of the Internet

HEAD - This code indicates that what follows is the header section of the Web page (anything in this section won't show on the main Web page when it is displayed).

TITLE - The title won't show on the main Web page either (because it is inside the HEAD section); however, the title will show at the top of your Web browser's screen and will be the name given to the Web page when someone bookmarks it. It will also be the name that shows up for the page when a search engine indexes it.

BODY - This section contains the headings, text and graphics that will actually be displayed on the Web browser when someone visits the Web page.

Figure 5 shows how Figure 4 looks when viewed by a Web browser. As you can see, the only thing that appears on the main window of the browser is the text that was in the "Body" section of the Web page document. In this case, the text in the "Title" section appears at the top of the browser window. See "Putting it All Together" in *Chapter 5*, starting on page 141 for more about creating Web pages.

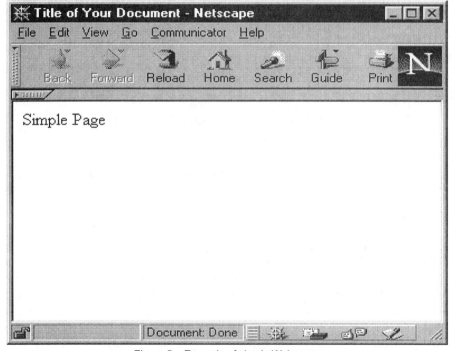

Figure 5: Example of simple Web page

Basic Web pages can be created with a simple text editor (programs such as NOTEPAD, WORDPAD, or WRITE). They can also be created in any basic word processor, but they must be saved as plain ASCII text files.

Web Editor Advantages

Web editors are software programs that are designed to create and modify HTML coded pages. There are many freeware, shareware, and commercial versions of Web editors available on the Internet. Commercial versions are also available at your local computer store. These Web editors range from full-featured commercial programs, to some very good shareware programs, to some very basic freeware programs.

Although Web pages can be created with any text editor or word processor, it won't be long before you discover that the process of manually adding HTML codes is very tedious. Web editors were developed to make this task faster and easier.

You can download samples of many Web editors from the Internet and try them out before you purchase them. You can find out which one you like before you spend a lot of money on it.

The HTML editor program I use is called HotDog Professional. It is a commercial program that is available on the Internet and gives you a free trial of the program before you buy it. Hot Dog Professional is a very highly rated program that allows you to create a basic Web page, as well as add many advanced features to your Web pages, with very little effort. A beginner version with less features, called HotDog Express, is also available.

Figure 6 shows an example of the types of shareware and freeware HTML programs available. Do not be alarmed by this large list of programs. You do not have to learn all of them in order to make Web pages. I suggest you download one from the Beginner category and try it for a while.

The Tucows shareware Web site contains many Web editors for Windows 95/98, Windows 3.x and Macintosh. This site also includes reviews of these software programs (with a 5-cow rating being best). Tucows is located at: **http://www.tucows.com/**.

HTML software at this site is in the following categories:
HTML Accessories
HTML Color Pickers
HTML Editors - Beginner
HTML Editors - Advanced
HTML Editors - Text
HTML Editors - Toolbar
HTML Editors - WYSIWYG
HTML Image Mappers
HTML Special Effects
HTML Validators

These programs range from full-featured Web editors to task specific programs, such as image mappers or validators. These programs can help the genealogist learn to create an effective Web site that others will want to visit.

Figure 6:   Tucows - HTML programs

Most of the shareware programs listed at the Tucows software site allow you to have a free trial period before you have to purchase them. If you find you do not like your first choice, download another and try that one for a while.

One of the major differences between using a Web editor, as opposed to a text editor, for creating your Web pages is how easy it is to put the correct HTML codes in the correct locations on the page. For example, to make the title of your Web page in the largest header size available:

- You must put <H1> before the title and </H1> after the title with a text editor

- You highlight the text and click your mouse button on the toolbar icon labeled <H1> with an HTML editor.

Most HTML editors can convert plain text files into HTML files with the HTML codes automatically placed where the formatting is needed. This way, if you have a text page in your word processor that you want to put on the Internet (such as a family story), you do not have to retype the pages to put them into HTML format. This saves much time and effort.

A Web editor also gives you the advantage of being able to insert hundreds of codes without having to look up their proper syntax in a reference book. You simply click on a button or a pull-down menu and choose the item you want to add to your page. The Web editor then inserts the proper codes. It won't be long before you will wonder why anyone would even consider using a text editor rather than an HTML Web editor.

Richard Says

There are a few features that I feel are very important in a Web editor. You will have to decide which features are the most important to you. I feel a Web editor should be easy to use. Another nice feature to have is a spell checker. You do not want to put a document with a misspelled word up on your Web site for the whole world to see.

Still another nice feature to have in a Web editor is HTML validation. This feature finds HTML coding mistakes on your page. This becomes increasingly important as your pages increase in complexity and have more coding in them.

Although you may never need to use many of the types of HTML tools that are available in Figure 6, this list is provided to let you know how much software is available to assist you with your Web page creation.

Alternative Methods

There are a few other ways of creating Web pages. One method is to use a standard word processor, while another is to use an integrated program such as Netscape Communicator.

Word Processor:

Modern word processing programs, such as WordPerfect 8 and Word 97, allow you to save standard text pages as Web pages. The programs will automatically insert the proper HTML codes to make the Web page layout look like the text page did. Simply follow these instructions:

- WordPerfect 8: From the "File" pull-down menu, select "Save As . . . " Under "File type" select HTML. Then give the file the name you wish and select "Save."

- Word 97: From the "File" pull-down menu, select "Save As . . ." Under "Save as type" select HTML Document. Then give the file the name you wish and select "Save."

Netscape Communicator:

With the Netscape Communicator program, you can take any Web page you like and use it as the basis for your own page.

- First, go to that page using Netscape Communicator.

- Select "Edit page" from the "File" pull-down menu (see Fig 7).

- The page will be loaded onto your computer in the Netscape Composer program (see Fig 8).

- When you have completed all of the modifications you want to make, save the page to your hard drive by selecting "Save As" from the "File" pull-down menu.

- Give the file the name you wish and select "Save."

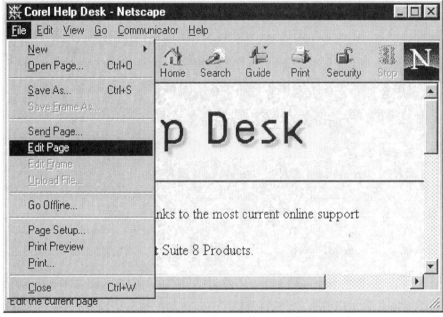

Figure 7:   Netscape Communicator - Edit Page

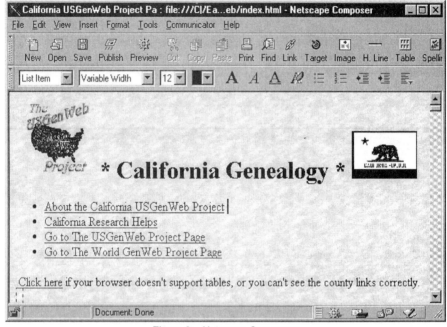

Figure 8: Netscape Composer

These alternative methods are so easy to use you may wonder why you would even want to use a Web editor. This is why they are good for beginners, or as a starting point. However, when you want more control over the way your Web pages look, then you will need a Web editor. You would also be able to add special graphics and other features not available with these alternative methods.

Genealogical
Data
Considerations

## Chapter 3

Creating a GEDCOM File

Many of the programs discussed in this book will require you to use a GEDCOM file. This chapter is divided into two sections: First, how to create a GEDCOM file with many of the popular commercial genealogy programs. Second, how to use the various utility programs available to remove information about living people from a GEDCOM file.

 GEDCOM stands for **GE**nealogical **D**ata **COM**munication. This is a standard format that was developed in the 1980's by The Church of Jesus Christ of Latter-day Saints. It allows the data that was entered into one genealogy program to be read and used by another genealogy or utility program. This enables you to use many different programs and take advantage of their different features. The GEDCOM standard has changed over the years and is currently at version 5.5. Genealogical computing has evolved to the point where GEDCOM needs further changes to be able to better support the multimedia features of the new genealogical software.

If your genealogy program does not offer you the ability to remove information about living people from your genealogical data, you may want to consider using one of the GEDCOM utility programs that will be covered in this chapter.

The following are steps used to create Web pages from a commercial software program after using one of the data removal programs to strip out the information about any people in your database who may be living.

- Create a GEDCOM file with your genealogy program.

- Process the GEDCOM file with the removal program of your choice.

- Create a new family file or database with your genealogy software program.

- Import the cleaned GEDCOM file into the new family file.

- Create your Web pages from this new family file

It is very easy to create a GEDCOM file with most genealogy programs. There is no way to explain here how every genealogy software program on the market today creates GEDCOM files, but most of the programs are very similar in the way they import and export GEDCOM files.

To use some of the shareware programs you download, you will need a decompression program, like Pkunzip for DOS, WinZip for Windows, or StuffIt Expander for Macintosh. These programs must be installed on your hard drive so you can decompress software that has been compressed for faster Internet transfer. See *Appendix B,* starting on page 289.

Following are some brief explanations of a few of the most commonly used genealogy programs that can create Web pages.

Ancestral Quest

The current program release is version 3.0. If you have an older version, an upgrade is available from The Hope Foundation. You can reach them at (800) 825-8864 or see their Web page at: **http://www.ancquest.com/**.

- From the main screen, select "Export . . ." from the "File" pull-down menu. The "GEDCOM Export" dialog box appears (see Figure 9).

- Select the type of GEDCOM file you want to create and the type of notes and information you want to include. Now click on the "Select . . ." button.

- When the "Select Set of Individuals" box appears (Figure 10), choose the records you want to include in your GEDCOM file. They can be chosen by name or by RIN number. You can also select their families, ancestors, descendants, etc.

- After you have made all your selections, click "OK." The "GEDCOM File Save As" box appears (Figure 11).

- Select the location and name of the file, then click "OK." The GEDCOM file will then be created.

Figure 9:   Ancestral Quest - GEDCOM Export

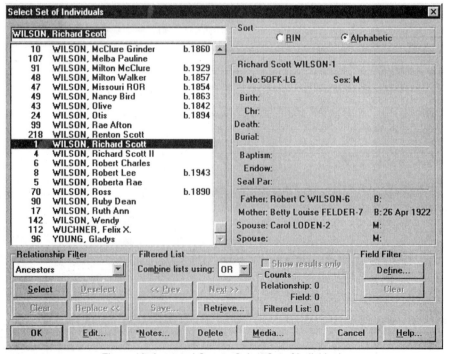

Figure 10: Ancestral Quest - Select Set of Individuals

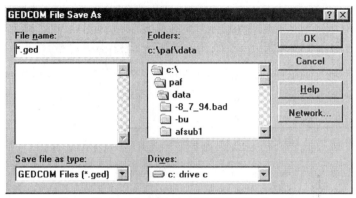

Figure 11: Ancestral Quest - GEDCOM File Save As

Family Origins

The current program release is version 7.01. If you have an older version, visit their Web site at: **http://www.parsonstech.com/**.

- From the main program screen select "Export GEDCOM..." in the "GEDCOM" section of the "File" pull-down menu.

- You will then see the "GEDCOM file to Create?" screen (see Figure 12).

Figure 12: Family Origins - GEDCOM file to create?

- Now select the destination drive, directory, and the name for the GEDCOM file you are going to create. Click on the "Save" button and the "GEDCOM Export" dialog box will appear (see Figure 13).

- Select the type of GEDCOM file you want to create (usually General), the notes you want to include, and the people you want to include.

- Click on the "OK" button. If you had highlighted the "Select people to export" option, the "Select People to Export" screen will appear (see Figure 14).

- From this screen, you can select the records you want included in the GEDCOM file: An individual, their family, ancestors, or descendants. When you have finished, click on the "<u>O</u>K" button.

- A GEDCOM progress box will appear as the file is created. When it is complete, you will be returned to the main program screen. Your GEDCOM file will have been saved with the name and location you selected from the "GEDCOM file to Create?" screen (see Figure 12).

Figure 13: Family Origins - GEDCOM Export

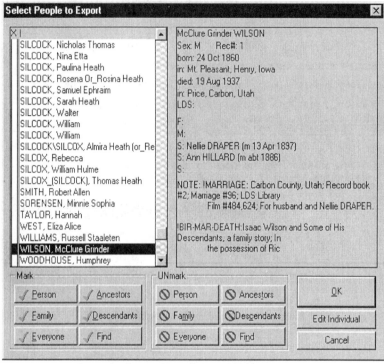

Figure 14: Family Origins - Select People to Export

Family Tree Maker

The current program release is version 5.0b. If you have an older version, you can order an upgrade by telephone at (800) 315-0672. For further information about upgrading see their Web site at: **http://www.familytreemaker.com/upgrdftw.html**.

Be aware that this program exports your entire database. It does NOT let you create a GEDCOM file containing only part of your database.

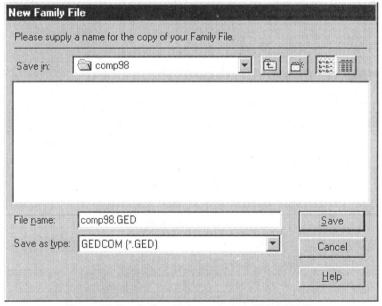

Figure 15: Family Tree Maker - create a GEDCOM file

- From the main program screen, select "Copy/Export Family File . . ." from the "File" pull-down menu. The screen shown in Figure 15 will appear.

- Click on the arrow beside the "Save in:" field and choose the drive and directory where you want the GEDCOM file saved.

- Type a name for the GEDCOM file in the "File name:" field.

- Click on the arrow beside the "Save as type" field and select GEDCOM (*.GED) from the drop-down menu.

- Click the "Save" button. The "Export to GEDCOM" screen appears (see Figure 16). Set the "File Type" section of this screen as shown in Figure 16 (Destination, GEDCOM and Character set). For your information, if you select "Indent records:," your GEDCOM file will be more readable in a word processing program. If you select "Abbreviate tags:," the program will use abbreviations for the GEDCOM tags, instead of the full tag names.

- Once you have made all your selections, click on the "OK" button. The GEDCOM file will be created and you will be returned to the main Family Tree Maker program screen.

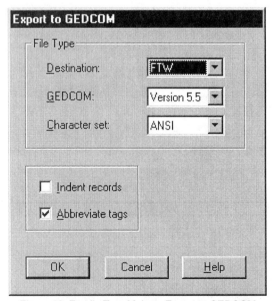

Figure 16: Family Tree Maker - Export to GEDCOM

Legacy

The current program release is version 2.0. When they update the program, they do not change the program's version number, only the build date of the program. The current build date is April 14, 1999. To find the build date of your program, select "General Information" from the "Help" pull-down menu of the main program screen and the "Build Date" will be displayed. Free program updates are available at **http://www.legacyfamilytree.com/**.

To create a GEDCOM file:

- From the main screen select "Export To" then "GEDCOM File" from the "File" pull-down menu. The "GEDCOM Export" dialog box will appear (see Figure 17).

- Select the type of GEDCOM file you want to create and the records you want to include in the file. There is even an option to "Suppress detail for Living people" and/or change the name fields of living people to indicate "Living."

- Click on the "Customize" button and the "Items to Include for GEDCOM for Legacy" screen appears (see Figure 18). Once you have selected your options, click the "OK" button and you will be returned to the "GEDCOM Export" screen.

- Click on the "Select File Name and Start Export" button. The "Export GEDCOM File" screen appears (see figure 19). From this screen, select the name and location where you want to save the GEDCOM file, then click on the "OK" button.

- The GEDCOM file will be saved. You will then get a message indicating the export of the GEDCOM file was complete.

- Click on the "OK" button and you will be returned to the Legacy main screen.

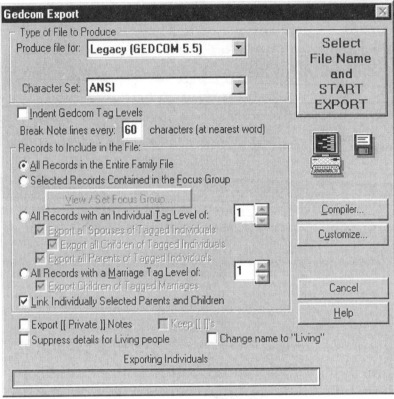

Figure 17: Legacy - GEDCOM Export

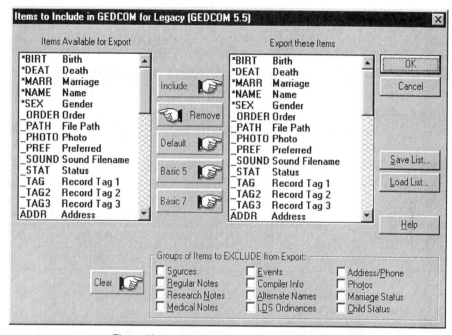

Figure 18: Legacy - Items to Include in GEDCOM

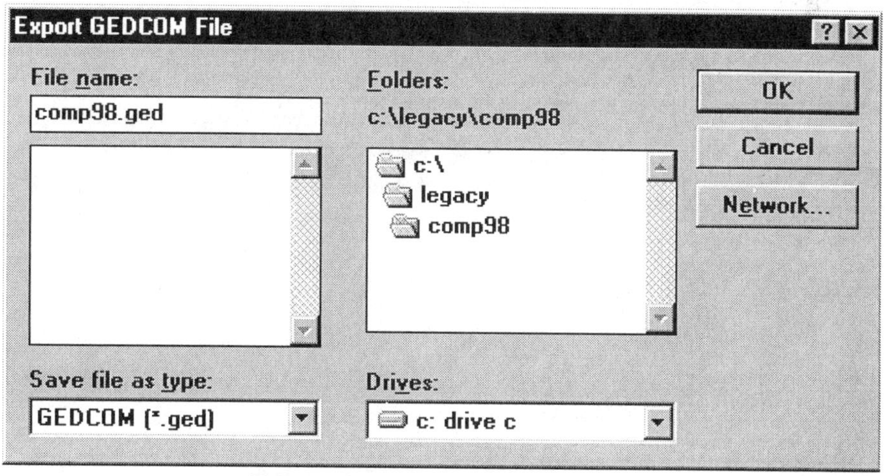

Figure 19: Legacy - Export GEDCOM File

Generations

Generations is a full-featured, commercial genealogy program. It is evolved from the Reunion program created by Leister Productions. Sierra Software produces the current version of the program, which is version 5.2 dated October 30, 1998. Their Internet Web site is located at: **http://www.sierra.com/sierrahome/familytree/**.

To create a GEDCOM file:

- From the main program screen, select "Import/Export" then "Export GEDCOM" from the "File" pull-down menu (see Figure 20).

- The GEDCOM Export screen will appear (see Figure 21).

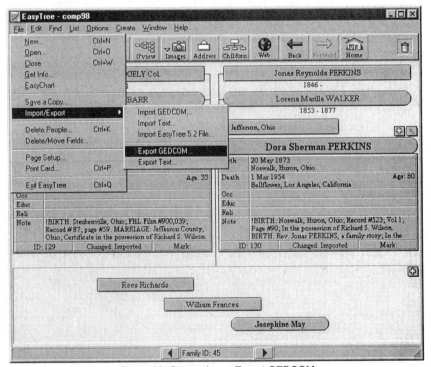

Figure 20: Generations - Export GEDCOM

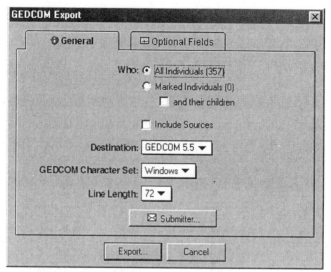

Figure 21: Generations - General tab

- From the General tab of the GEDCOM Export screen, you can select the type of GEDCOM file you want to create, which records you want to include in the file, and you can modify your information with the submitter button. You can also select the Optional Fields tab and make further choices about which fields to include in the GEDCOM creation (see Figure 22). You can keep any data from being exported. To do this, simply click the mouse button the remove the X from each of the boxes under the Export column for all the data you want to exclude.

- Once you have made all of your selections, click on the Export button. You will then see the Save GEDCOM File screen in Figure 23. Give the file a name and click on the Save button. The program will then save the GEDCOM file with the options you had selected.

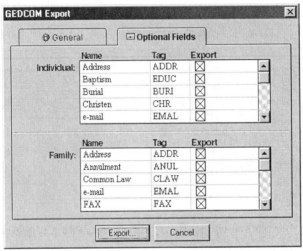

Figure 22: Generations - Optional Fields tab

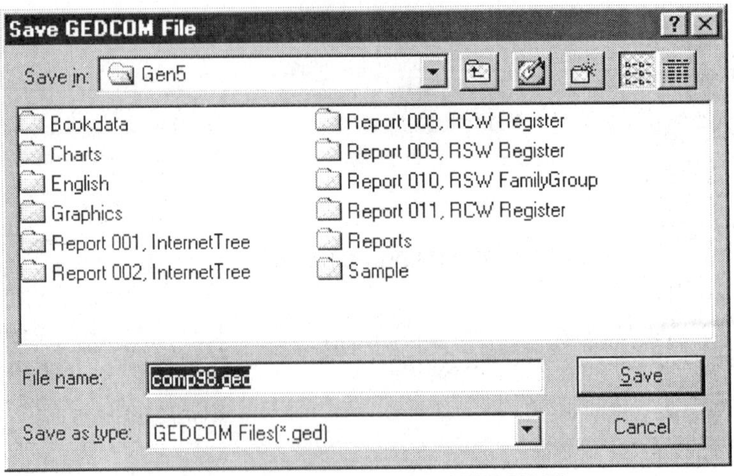

Figure 23: Generations - Save GEDCOM File

The Master Genealogist

The current program version is 3.7. If you have an older version, check their Web site at **http://www.whollygenes.com/** for upgrades and more information.

To create a GEDCOM file:

- From the main screen, select "File" from the pull-down menu, then select "Data Set," then "Export to . . ." then click on "GED-GEDCOM" (see Figure 24).

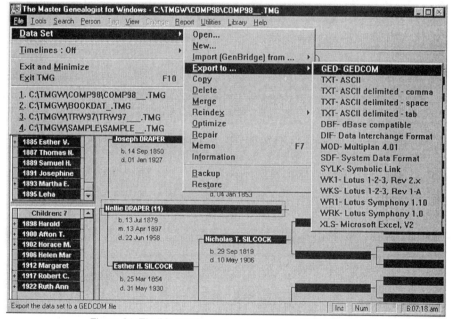

Figure 24: The Master Genealogist - create a GEDCOM file

- The Custom Report Writer screen will appear (see Figure 25).

- Click on the "Use this sample" button and you will see the "Report Definition - GEDCOM Export" screen (Figure 26).

- Select the information and style of the data you want to include in your GEDCOM file by making selections from the screens on each of the three tabs.

- From the "Options" tab you can select "Suppress details for living individuals." If this option is chosen, then all name and event tags are suppressed for people for with LIVING=Y (see Figure 27).

- Once you have made your selections, click on the "Generate" button (see Figure 26) and the GEDCOM file will be created.

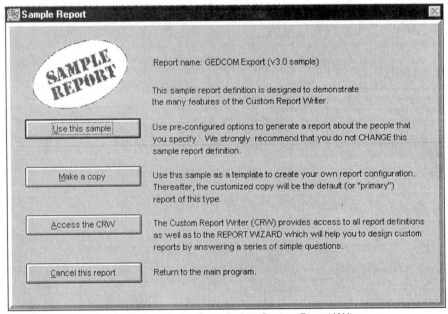

Figure 25: The Master Genealogist - Custom Report Writer

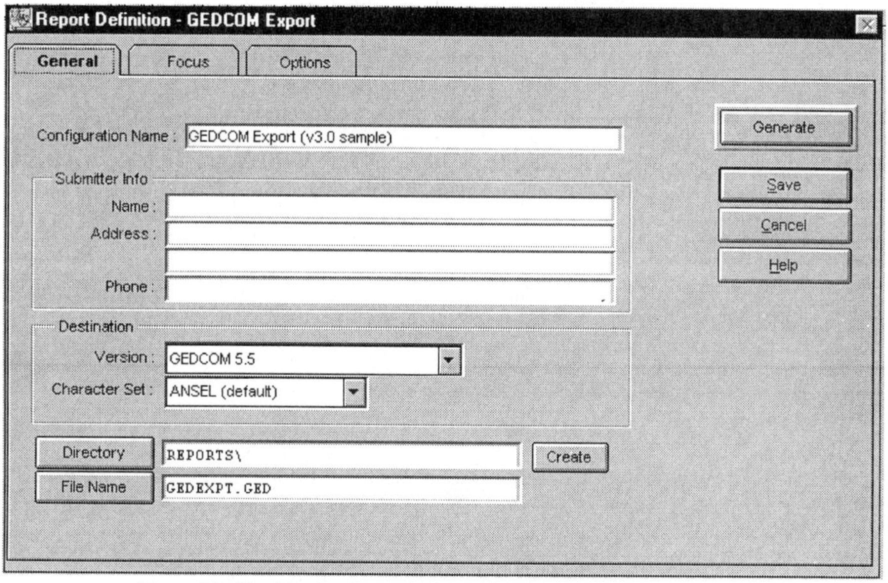

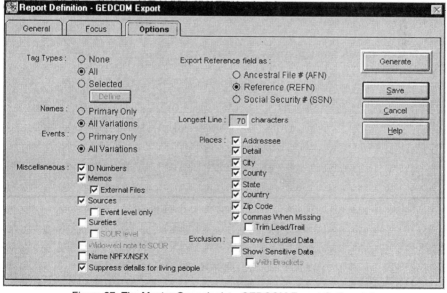

Figure 26: The Master Genealogist - GEDCOM Export General tab

Figure 27: The Master Genealogist - GEDCOM Export Options tab

Ultimate Family Tree

The current program version is 2.9. If you have an older version of Ultimate Family Tree, Family Gathering, Roots IV or Roots V, you may want to consider an upgrade. They are at **http://www.uftree.com/**.

To create a GEDCOM file:

- From the main screen, select "Save <u>A</u>s" from the "<u>F</u>ile" pull-down menu. The "Save As" screen appears (see Figure 28).

- Click on the down arrow next to the "Save file as type" field and select "GEDCOM." Change the drive and directory to the location where you want to save the GEDCOM file. Enter a file name with the extension of *.ged.*

- Click on the "OK" button and the "Save As GEDCOM Options" screen will open (see Figure 29).

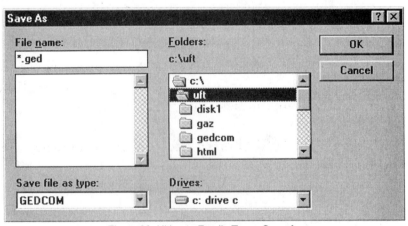

Figure 28: Ultimate Family Tree - Save As

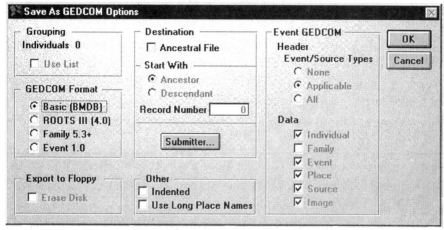

Figure 29: Ultimate Family Tree - Save As GEDCOM Options

- From this screen, you can determine what the format and content of the GEDCOM file will be. If you want to export only part of your project, you need to use the "Use List" option under "Individuals" in the "Grouping" section (see Figure 29). This option will only work if you have previously made your grouping list (for more on Grouping Lists, see your program manual).

- Once you have selected the options you want, click on the "OK" button. The GEDCOM file will then be created and a message will appear indicating the export was completed.

- Click on the "OK" button and you will be returned to the main program screen.

Privacy Issues

You may want to consider what type of personal information you want to include on your Web pages. Sometimes living people do not want their data placed on a Web site for the whole world to see. Some conversion programs do not have the option of excluding information about living persons; however, there are other programs available that will take care of this problem. These programs automate the process of stripping out personal information about living individuals from any GEDCOM file. Following is a discussion about some of these programs.

This section of the book is also helpful if you share genealogical data with other people. Normally, you convert information stored in your genealogy program into the GEDCOM format so that people with different genealogy programs can use the data. Use one of the programs mentioned in this section to remove information about living people from the GEDCOM file you have created. Then you can send it off to other researchers, or place it on the Web, without worrying about any sensitive information being included.

Never rely entirely on any of these programs. Carefully review results to be sure they removed all the data you wanted. There may be information you wanted removed that they were not programmed to find.

GEDClean

GEDClean version 2.11, dated January 31, 1998, is a freeware program for Windows 3.x, Windows 95/98 or NT. It is available for downloading at **http://www.raynorshyn.com/gedclean/**. You can contact the author, Tom Raynor at *TechSupport@RaynOrShyn.com*.

This program removes all information about living people, except their name (unless you chose the option to also exclude the names of living people) and their relationship to other names in the database (parent, spouse, child). It adds a note which states "Living Individual–Details Withheld."

You will need to know a few basic DOS commands in order to install and use this program. (See the "Basic DOS Commands" section in *Appendix B*, starting on page 281).

To install the GEDClean program:

1. Download the GEDClean program from the Internet.

2. Create a directory or folder on your computer's hard drive (i.e., C:\GEDClean).

3. Copy *GEDCle01.exe* into the directory you just created.

4. From DOS, or in a DOS window, change to the directory you created (type CD C:\Gedclean).

5. Type *GEDCle01* and press Enter to unzip the files.

6. This will expand (unzip) several files into that directory.

To run the GEDClean program:

- From Windows File Manager or Windows Explorer, navigate to the directory that GEDClean is in.

- Double-click on the "GEDClean" or "GEDClean.exe" file.

- You can also drag the file to your desktop to create an icon for the program, then all you have to do is click on the icon to start the program.

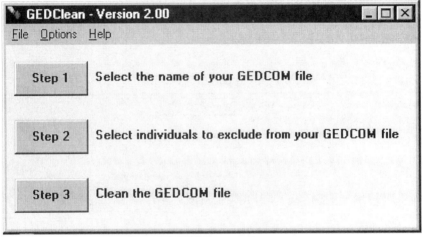

Figure 30: GEDClean - main screen

- From the opening screen (see Figure 30), select the "Options" pull-down menu (see Figure 31).

- From the "Options" screen, set a tag that will indicate that a person is still alive (the default tag is !ALIVE). You set the number of years before a person is considered dead, if their death information is not entered. You also have the option of withholding their name as well as their data.

- Once you have set the options you desire, click on the "OK" button, which will return you to the main screen.

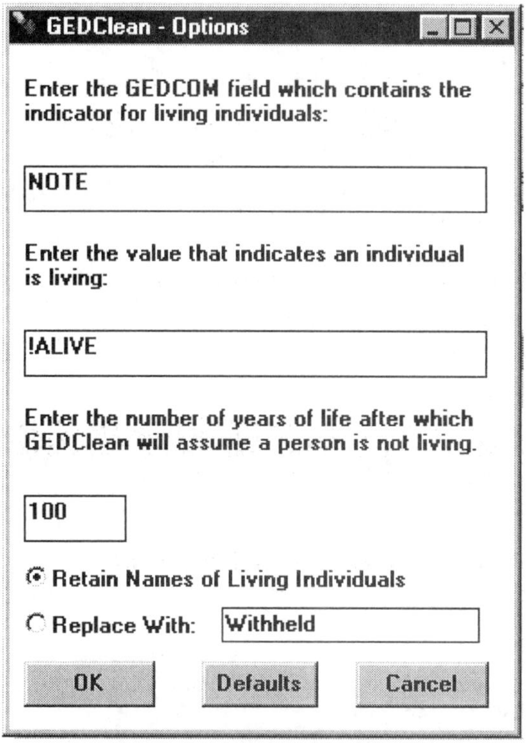

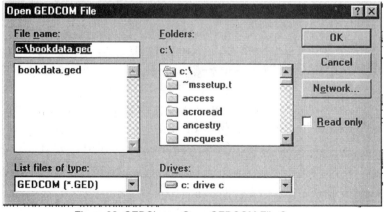

Figure 31: GEDClean - Options

Figure 32: GEDClean - Open GEDCOM File Screen

• From the main screen (Figure 30), click on the "Step 1" button. The "Open GEDCOM File" window appears (see Figure 32).

• Enter the name and location of the GEDCOM file you want to convert and click the "OK" button. This will take you back to the main screen again.

• Click on the "Step 2" button. The "Select Living Individuals" screen will appear (see Figure 33).

• You now have three options to chose from. If you select "Option 3," the "Unknown Status" screen appears (see Figure 34). Select either "Living Individual - exclude details," or "Not Living - OK to retain details" and click on the "OK" button.

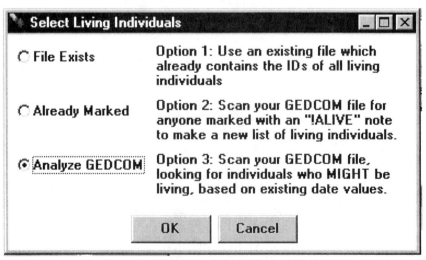

Figure 33: GEDClean - Select Living Individuals

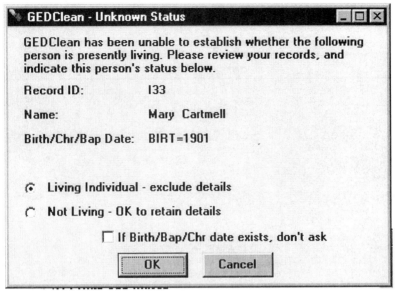

Figure 34: GEDClean - Unknown Status

- Once you select the "OK" button, the program will show you the next individual who does not fit the criteria you set. This process will continue until all the people with "Unknown Status" are entered. You must manually decide whether or not to suppress each individual's data. Once completed, you will be returned to the main screen. This process creates a text file named *filename.txt* with the same filename and in the same directory as your GEDCOM file (*filename.ged*).

- Select "Step 3" from the main GEDClean window. The program then cleans the information from your GEDCOM file and saves a new GEDCOM file with the same name as the original GEDCOM file. Your unmodified GEDCOM file (the original GEDCOM file containing the data about the living people) is saved as *filename.old*.

The new GEDCOM file that does not contain the data about living individuals will have the same name as the GEDCOM file you started with (*filename.ged*).

GEDPrivy

GEDPrivy version 1.01, dated September 19, 1997, is a shareware program for Windows 3.x or Windows 95. It is used to create privacy for data in genealogy files (GEDCOM files). GEDPrivy is available for downloading on the Internet at **http://members.aol.com/gedprivy/**. The registration fee is $10 (US). You can contact the author, John L. Goodwin, at *GedPrivy@aol.com*.

Figure 35: About GEDPrivy

GEDPrivy's features include:
- Makes the birth data of living people "Private"
- Automatic selection—no need to manually pick and choose individual family members
- Option to remove sources for living persons
- Compatible with genealogy programs via GEDCOM
- Windows 95/98 version supports long file names

If you register this program, you will never have to pay for any future upgrades. Your support will allow the author to improve the program, particularly as users request more features.

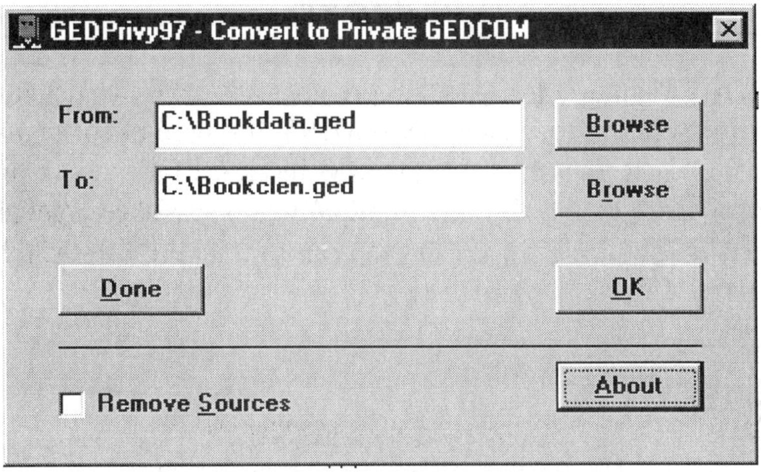

Figure 36: GEDPrivy - Convert to Private GEDCOM

- When you start the program, the "Convert to Private GEDCOM" screen appears (see Figure 36).

- Type the name of the GEDCOM file you want to convert in the "From:" box.

- In the "To:" box, type the name you want the new GEDCOM file to have. The program also gives you the option of removing the source notes from the individuals who are living by selecting the "Remove Sources" box.

- Click the "OK" button. The program will run and, when complete, you will see a message indicating the conversion was complete.

- Press the "OK" button.

Once this process is complete, your GEDCOM file will contain the word "Private" for everyone with no death date or who is under 100 years old. Birth places and marriage information for these people are not removed.

Res Prívata

Res Privata Version 1.0.1 (32 bit), dated June 13, 1998, is a shareware program for Windows 95/98/NT. A 16 bit version is also available for Windows 3.x. It is written by Naiborly Software. Their e-mail address is *<naibor@ozemail.com.au>*. You can download the program at **http://www.ozemail.com.au/~naibor/**.

Res Privata removes private data about living people from your genealogy GEDCOM file. Not only does it remove details of birth, marriage, divorce and adoption, but it will allow you to control exactly which details to leave in or take out. Because it is a Windows 95/98-based program, it also supports long file names.

Res Privata keeps your original GEDCOM file intact by creating a new filtered copy. GEDCOM files created with Res Privata can be used with popular GEDCOM-to-HTML translators, or put back into your commercial genealogy program in order to create HTML files for publishing on the Internet.

Res Privata works with standard release 5.5 GEDCOM files. It has been tested with GEDCOM files created by quite a few genealogy programs.

This program is now available with an automated setup program. With this program it can automatically create its own icon and folder for Windows 95/98/NT.

Here are the steps to install this program:

- Create a directory or folder on your hard drive where you will place the file you have downloaded (i.e., *rpriv32i.zip*).

- Copy the file (*rpriv32.zip*) into the folder you have created.

- Unzip the file into that directory or folder (see "Compression Programs" in *Appendix B*, page 289).

- An icon for the program will be automatically created in a folder off of the start button in Windows 95/98.

Figure 37: Res Privata - main screen

To run the Res Privata program:

- Click on the icon for the program and the main screen appears (see Figure 37).

- Select the GEDCOM file from which you want to remove information. To do this, click on the "Set Options" button.

- From the "Files" tab on the "Res Privata Options" screen (see Figure 38), enter the name of the GEDCOM file and the name of the output file (the cleaned file). If you need to browse for the files, click on the " . . ." button to the right of each field. You can also create or use an options file if you would like to use the same options over again.

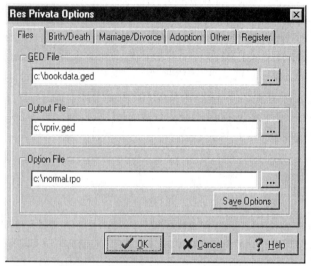

Figure 38: Res Privata Options - Files tab

- Figure 39 shows the "Birth/Death" tab and the options available for the removal of birth and death data from your file. You can also select other data you want to have removed by selecting the corresponding tabs at the top of the box.

- The "Other" tab allows options for other types of data you want to remove from your GEDCOM file (see Figure 40).

- If you want to use the same options for more than one GEDCOM file, you can save them by selecting the "Save Options" button from the "Files" tab screen (see Figure 38). Once you have selected all your options, select the "OK" button and you will be returned to the main screen.

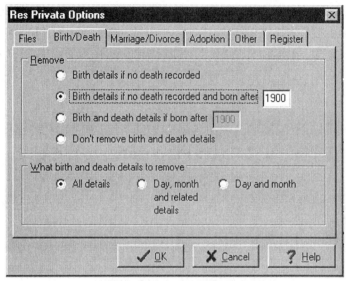

Figure 39: Res Privata - Birth/Death tab

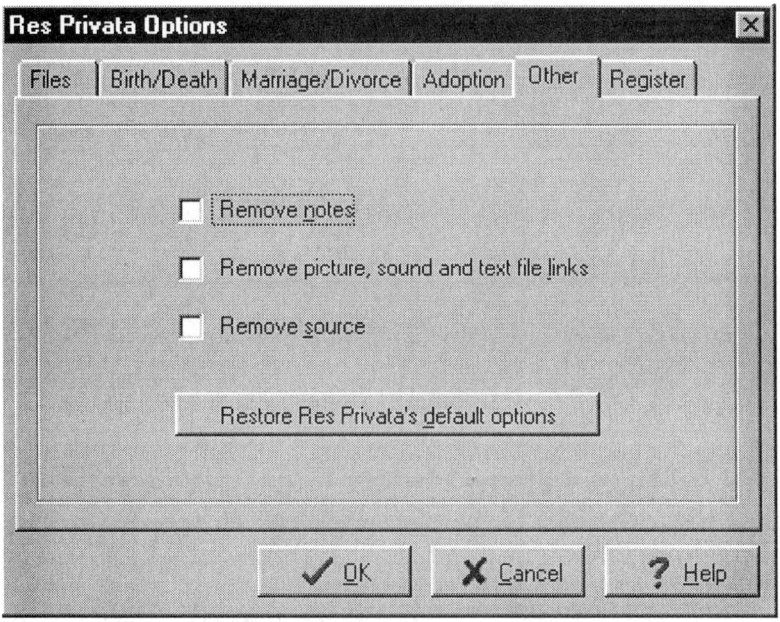

Figure 40: Res Privata - Other tab

- From the main screen, select the "Filter GED File" button to start the removal process. Once the process is complete, the screen will show you a summary of the processing it did (see Figure 41).

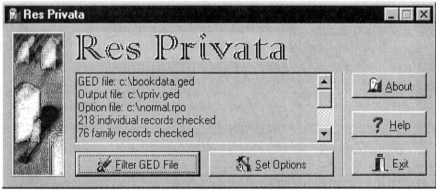

Figure 41: Rev Privata - summary screen

Converting Genealogical Data in Minutes

## Chapter 4

Pros and Cons of Manual vs Automatic

While you can manually create a few Web pages for a small amount of data on a small family tree, you will find it is a very large job to manually set up Web pages for hundreds (or thousands) of family members. That is where automatic conversion programs come in. You can generate hundreds of Web pages for thousands of people in just a few minutes with such a program.

Automatic conversion programs are software programs that were created to take your genealogy data (from your genealogy program or a GEDCOM file) and convert that data into HTML pages suitable for presentation on the World Wide Web. These conversion programs only work with data you have put into a genealogy database program or exported from a genealogy database program in GEDCOM format.

The disadvantage to using an automatic conversion program is that you have one more piece of software to learn to use. Unless, of course, you are already using a genealogy software program that includes an automatic conversion feature (such as Ultimate Family Tree or Family Origins).

Richard
Says

I would recommend setting up just your home page and a few additional information pages manually. Then, let an automatic conversion program take care of the tedious task of converting all of your genealogical data to be placed on additional Web pages on your Web site.

Automatic Conversion Process

 Do not try to read straight through this chapter in one sitting. Trying to digest the whole chapter at once may result in indigestion of the brain. Conversion programs can be quite complex. Do not try to understand all of them at once. Find one that creates Web pages the way you would like to have them, then concentrate on learning just that program.

If you decide to use the automatic conversion process, all you need to do is decide which software program you like best. First, you need to evaluate what type of data you want on your Web pages. You also need to consider how much space you can afford to have your Web pages use. Most Internet space providers have space limits and charge you for additional space above that limit. Remember, the more space your pages need, the more it may cost you.

Next, select the records you want to have on your Web pages. You may want to have several different smaller sets of data for the different family lines you are researching. In other words, you may want one set of Web pages with all the descendants of John Milton WILSON, and then another set of pages with all the ancestors of Josephine May FELDER. You can create as many sets of Web pages as you like or have room for.

Now look at the conversion program you chose. If the program is a GEDCOM-to-HTML conversion program, you will need to create a GEDCOM file of the data you have selected from your genealogy program (see "Creating a GEDCOM File" section of *Chapter 3*, starting on page 29). The GEDCOM file needs to include all of the individuals you want on your Web pages. There are many shareware or freeware programs available that can create Web pages from a generic GEDCOM file or Personal Ancestral File (PAF) database.

If the program you chose is a full-featured genealogy program that creates Web pages, you would not need to create a GEDCOM file. These software programs include the ability to create Web pages directly from your data. You just select the people you wish to include on your pages. Some even allow you to include photographs and graphics on the Web pages they create for you.

Not all conversion programs will be covered here. Sufficient examples of shareware, freeware, and commercial conversion programs are given here to get you started. Be sure you check out the feature comparison charts on pages 138, 139.

Check out the **http://www.compuology.com/richard/compare.htm** Web site. This is my personal Web site where I have put much of my own genealogical data—using different genealogy and conversion programs. You can view the differences in the way the Web pages look when created with each program.

This chapter covers the step-by-step process of using these programs, which are all for IBM compatible computers. Many of them require the Windows or Windows 95/98 operating systems.

Macintosh owners can use the Sparrowhawk program, which is the Mac version of the GED2HTML conversion program. You can go to **http://www.tjp.washington.edu/bdm/genealogy/sparrowhawk.html** to download it. There are also a few Macintosh genealogy software programs available that can create Web pages directly from your genealogy database.

Ancestral Quest

Ancestral Quest is a full-featured commercial genealogy program. It is available from The Hope Foundation. The latest version of the program is version 3.0. You can reach them at (800) 825-8864 or see their Web page at: **http://www.ancquest.com/**.

The steps required to create Web pages:

- Select the *Tools* pull-down menu.

- Select *Create Web Page...* from that menu. This opens the Web Page Wizard's selection box (see Figure 42).

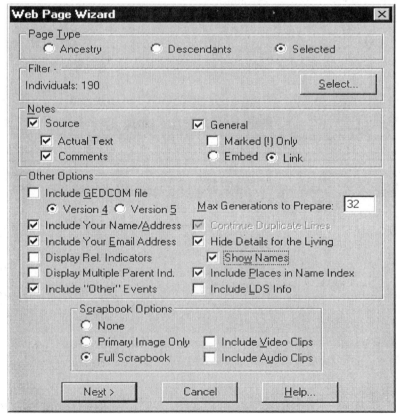

Figure 42: Ancestral Quest - Web Page Wizard

- Select all of the options for the Web creation process from this wizard. Select the individual you want to start with, whether you want ancestors or descendants, and what notes you wish to include. You have the option of including photographs, video, and/or audio clips associated with that person. You can also choose to exclude information about living people.

- Once you have made your selections, select the "Ne<u>x</u>t >" button. You will see the dialog box in Figure 43.

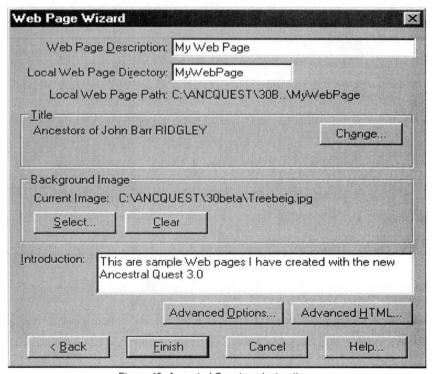

Figure 43: Ancestral Quest - select options

- Select the name and location of your new Web page, along with the title, background image, and introductory text.

- Select the "Advanced HTML ..." button to design custom headers and footers (see Figure 44).

- When you are finished, click on the "OK" button to go back to the screen in Figure 43.

- Click on the "Finish" button.

- Once the Web pages have all been created, you will see a dialog box that tells you the program has completed the Web pages. Select the "OK" button to continue.

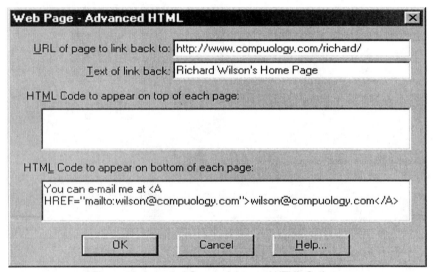

Figure 44: Ancestral Quest - Advanced HTML Options

Figures 45 and 46 are examples of Web pages created by the Ancestral Quest program.

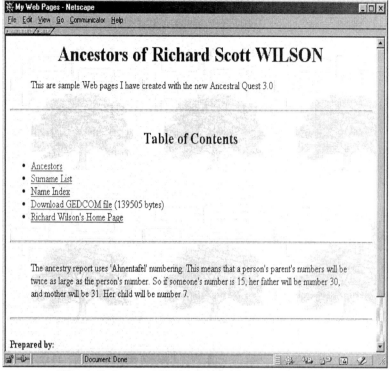

Figure 45: Ancestral Quest - Table of Contents Web page

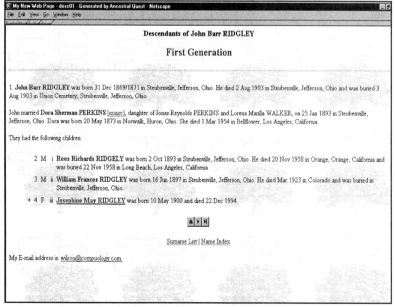

Figure 46: Ancestral Quest - sample Descendant Web page

Family Origins

Family Origins is a full-featured commercial genealogy software program. It creates Web pages that are good looking, as well as functional. It allows you to create either descendant or pedigree family histories. It will automatically include photographs you have entered into the program. Because this program does not hide information for living people, you must carefully choose what you include in the family history. You should also be aware that this program does not allow you to create custom headers or footers on the Web pages it creates.

The latest version of the program is 7.01, dated September 15, 1998. Information about the program is found at the following Web page: **http://www.parsonstech.com/**.

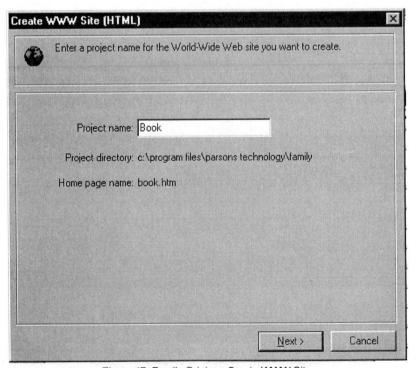

Figure 47: Family Origins - Create WWW Site

To create Web pages:

- Select "Create Web site" from the "Tools" pull-down menu. You will then see the box shown in Figure 47.

- Type in the name of the Web site you will be creating. Then select the "Next >" button.

- From the next dialog box (Figure 48), select the type of Web site you will be creating. You can select ancestors, descendants, or people you want to have included. From this screen you can also type an introductory paragraph to be included at the top of the main Web page.

- Once you have made your selections, click on the "Next >" button. The dialog box in Figure 49 will appear.

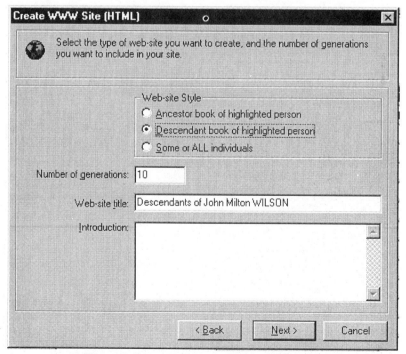

Figure 48: Family Origins - Select data for Web site

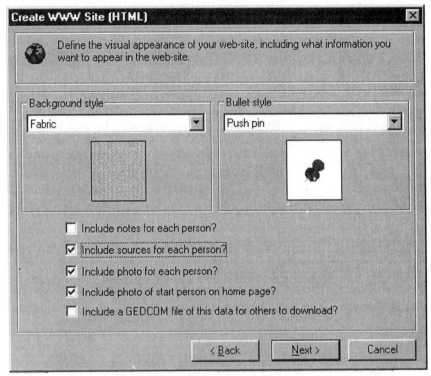

Figure 49: Family Origins - selection screen

- Select the type of graphic that will be used for the background, as well as the bullet style. You also select whether the pages will include notes, sources, or photographs. You can also have the program create a GEDCOM file of the corresponding data. When finished, click on the "Next >" button.

One very nice feature of this software is that it puts only the word "photo" next to the individual's information. This way a person viewing the Web page will not have to wait for all the photos on the page to load. If they decide to, they can view any photo by clicking on the word "photo."

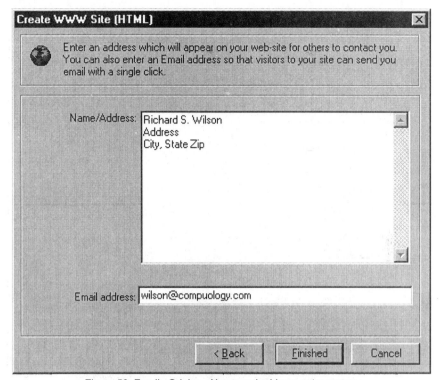

Figure 50: Family Origins - Name and address entry screen

- This is where you can enter the name, address, and e-mail address that you want to appear on the Web pages (see Figure 50). Once you have entered this, select the "**Finished**" button. The message "Generating WWW Site" will appear as the program counts through the generations while creating the pages.

- Once complete, the "Website Created" screen will appear (see Figure 51). This message indicates that the Web pages have been created. It gives you the location of where the files have been stored on your hard drive. In this example, the files were saved in the following location: **c:\program files\parsons technology\family origins\data\book\.**

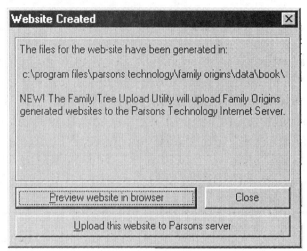

Figure 51: Family Origins - Website Created

If you select the "Preview website in browser" button, the program will start your Web browser software and load the main Web page it just created (see Figure 52). This gives you the opportunity to check out the pages before you upload them to your Internet space provider.

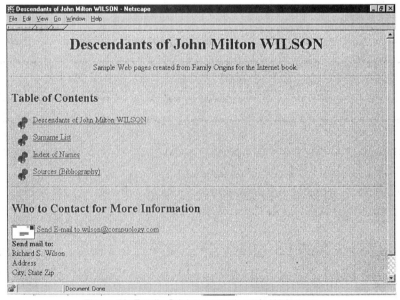

Figure 52: Family Origins - sample main Web page

Family Tree Maker

This is a full-featured commercial genealogy software program that is available for Windows or Macintosh. Family Tree Maker operates a little differently than the other programs reviewed here. It can only create Web pages from your data on the Internet, not on your computer. Your genealogical data is automatically uploaded to Family Tree Maker's Web site. You will <u>not</u> be able to create Web pages, using this program, which can be uploaded to other Web sites.

> Before uploading data to <u>any</u> Web site, make sure you read all the disclaimers and requirements for putting data on the site.

The current version of Family Tree Maker is 5.0b, dated August 7, 1998. You will find the Web page with more information located at: **https://www.familytreemaker.com/ftmvers.html.**

Richard Says:

If you would like to see an example of a home page on their Web site, check my page at **http://www.familytreemaker.com/users/w/i/l/Richard-S-Wilson/.**

Family Tree Maker has the ability to create a very unique Web page that uses Java, called InterneTree.

To create this report on their Web site:

- Select "<u>P</u>ublish Family Tree to the Internet . . ." from the <u>I</u>nternet pull-down menu. The screen in figure 53 appears.

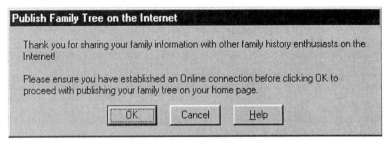

Figure 53: Family Tree Maker - Publish Family Tree

- Once you verify you are connected to the Internet, you select "OK."

- From the dialog box in Figure 54, click on the "Individuals to Include . . . " button. The dialog box in Figure 55 will come up. Once you have selected all the individuals you want to include, click on the "OK" button.

- You will be returned to the screen in Figure 53. Select the "OK" button. You will see a message indicating your report was uploaded and will be available online in 15 minutes.

- Once you have completed this process, you can go to your Web home page and click on the InterneTree link.

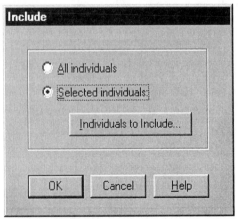

Figure 54: Family Tree Maker - Include individuals

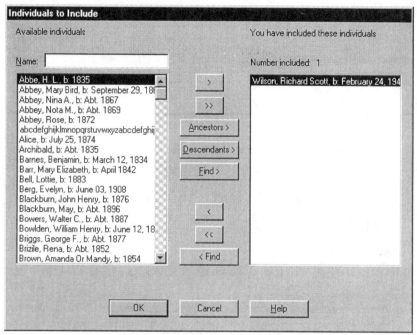

Figure 55: Family Tree Maker - Individuals to Include

The Web page will then be downloaded from Family Tree Maker Online (see Figure 56). This page includes a window in which the Java applet (program) runs. The Java applet displays your data in a pedigree format. The Web page includes instructions on how to move about in the window, resize it, and bring up a search list to find an individual's name.

Because this Web page uses Java, it will only work with a Web browser that is Java-enabled. Also, the entire file must be download in order for it to be displayed. This means that the visitor's computer must have enough speed, memory, and storage space available in order to display the Web page.

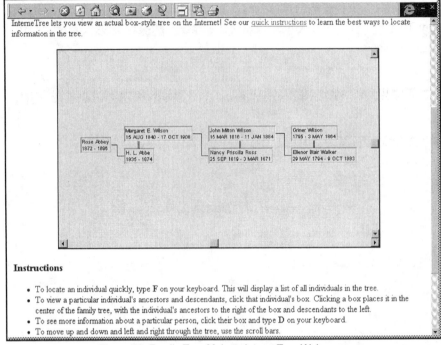

Figure 56: Family Tree Maker - InterneTree Web page

What is unique about this Web page is that a person can click on an individual on the pedigree, press the "D" key, and a detail of that individual will appear (see Figure 57). When you click on the "OK" button you will be returned to the screen in Figure 56.

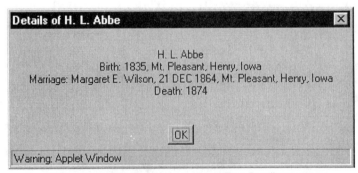

Figure 57: Family Tree Maker - InterneTree Details screen

From the Pedigree Web view (Figure 56), you can also press the "F" key and a list of everyone in the online database will be displayed (see Figure 58).

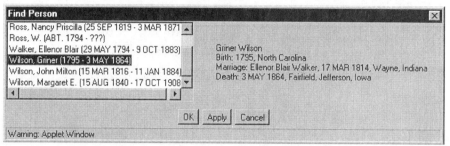

Figure 58: Family Tree Maker - InterneTree Find Person screen

If you select the "OK," or "Apply" button, the person you have highlighted will become the primary person on the main screen (Figure 56).

GED2HTM

GED2HTM is a shareware GEDCOM-to-HTML conversion program that generates Web pages in a cascading pedigree chart format. Its charts are almost identical to those generated by the Personal Ancestral File (PAF) genealogy program; however, the charts created by GED2HTM put all of the notes on separate pages that follow the pedigree charts. This program does not allow photos or graphics to be added to your Web pages.

GED2HTM was written by John Smith *<jsmithii@primenet.com>*. It is a GEDCOM-based program that creates Web pages in either DOS or Unix. The current version is 2.01, dated April 11, 1995. It is available for free on the Internet. It can be downloaded from **http://table.jps.net/~johns1/#gedpaf**.

The file you download is called *gedhtm03.zip*. It is in a compressed format that will need to be expanded, or unzipped, before it can be used. (See "Compression Programs" in *Appendix B*, starting on page 289 for more on how to zip and unzip files.) To use this program, you will need to know a little about DOS commands (see the "Basic DOS Commands" section of *Appendix B*, starting on page 281).

To install the program:

1. Create a directory or folder for GED2HTM (such as **C:\GED2HTM**).

2. Move the GED2HTM program files into the folder or directory you have created—after extracting them from the zip file.

3. Place the GEDCOM you created into that same directory or folder. (See "Creating a GEDCOM File" in Chapter 3, starting on page 29, for more information on creating GEDCOM files).

4. You can modify the following files with a text editor:

File Name	File Function
PED_HDR.TXT	Header for each HTML file
PED_TAIL.TXT	Footer for each HTML file
NDX_HDR.TXT	Header for the index HTML file
NDX_TAIL.TXT	Footer for the index HTML file

5. To run the GED2HTM program, you must be at a DOS prompt (the C:\> prompt). Type GED2HTM, then a space and then the name of the GEDCOM file (*filename.GED*) and press **Enter**. (If you just type **GED2HTM h** and press **Enter**, you will see the command options available for running this program).

The files mentioned in step 4 above make it possible for you to have custom headers and footers on each Web page. When you first install the program, they will contain the name and e-mail address of John Smith (the author of this program). You need to put in your own name and e-mail address. He puts his data in these files as a place holder so you will know where to put your data. You can also add other important items on each page, such as the address of your main Web page and a copyright notice, if you wish. You can see one of the unmodified files (*Ped_tail.txt*) in Figure 59.

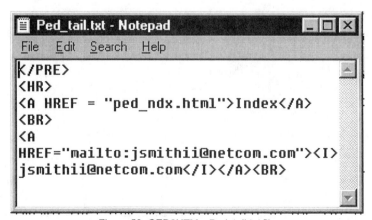

Figure 59: GED2HTM - *Ped_tail.txt* file

Options for running the GED2HTM program:

-r   Starting RIN 1   (Person to create a pedigree of)

-s   Start spouse RIN 0 (Spouse's RIN number)

-S   Number for the first pedigree chart (default is 1)

-C   Number of continuation chart (default is 2)

-m   Maximum generations to chart (default is 32767)

-f   Letters the HTML file names start with (default is ped)

        (i.e., *ped_001.htm*)

These options are selected by typing them after the GED2HTM command and before the GEDCOM filename. Typing **GED2HTM -r7 RICHARD.GED** will start the program and create a pedigree chart with RIN number 7 as the starting person on chart number 1. Be sure that you include the *.ged* after the GEDCOM file name. The program then lists the options it was told to use and creates the HTML files (see Figure 60).

C:\GED2HTM>*ged2htm -r7 richard.ged*
Generating chart with options:
"r" Start rin 7
"s" Start spouse rin 0
"S" Starting chart number 1
"C" Contining chart number 2
"m" Maximum generations to follow 32767
"f" html file names start with ped
Indexing richard.ged

Chart 040 Position 03   Margaret Williams
Sorting index file

C:\GED2HTM>

Figure 60: GED2HTM - sample operation

This program will assign Record Identification Numbers (RIN) numbers in the order that people are found in the GEDCOM file (Note: These RIN numbers may not be the same numbers that were in your original genealogy database).

All of the files created by GED2HTM end with the *.htm* extension, but all of the links it creates to other pages have the *.html* extension. You will have to manually rename all the files or the links won't work.

This program creates simple Web pages containing cascading pedigree charts with very little actual data; consequently, they take up very little space. This saves you from having to pay for extra Web space if your Web server only gives you a small amount of space for storing your Web pages.

Figure 61 shows a sample Web page created by the GED2HTM program.

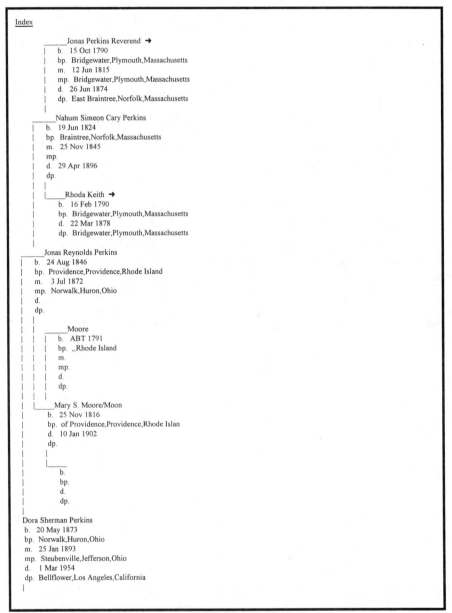

Figure 61: GED2HTM - sample Web page

GED2HTML

GED2HTML is a shareware conversion program written by Gene Stark. The latest version is 3.5e, dated September 26, 1998. The registration cost is $20.00 and includes free upgrades for two years. You can download it at **http://www.gendex.com/ged2html/**. This program creates good looking Web pages and allows graphics and photographs, though they must be linked manually. It does not have the ability to hide information on living people.

The GED2HTML program uses templates to create Web pages so that the format of the HTML files can be modified by the user. The template that comes with the program is named *standard.g2h*. It has comments throughout its listing that explain what the various portions of the template do. (See Figure 62).

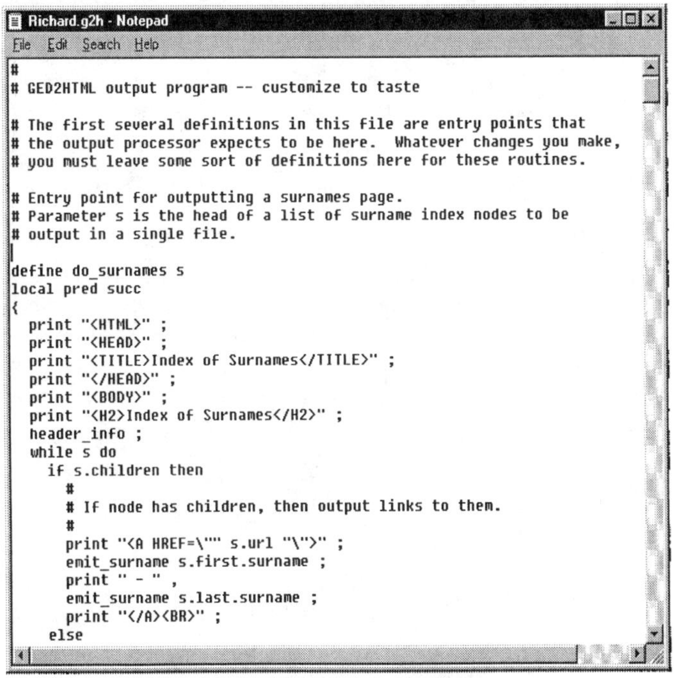


```
#
# GED2HTML output program -- customize to taste

# The first several definitions in this file are entry points that
# the output processor expects to be here.  Whatever changes you make,
# you must leave some sort of definitions here for these routines.

# Entry point for outputting a surnames page.
# Parameter s is the head of a list of surname index nodes to be
# output in a single file.

define do_surnames s
local pred succ
{
  print "<HTML>" ;
  print "<HEAD>" ;
  print "<TITLE>Index of Surnames</TITLE>" ;
  print "</HEAD>" ;
  print "<BODY>" ;
  print "<H2>Index of Surnames</H2>" ;
  header_info ;
  while s do
    if s.children then
      #
      # If node has children, then output links to them.
      #
      print "<A HREF=\"" s.url "\">" ;
      emit_surname s.first.surname ;
      print " - " ,
      emit_surname s.last.surname ;
      print "</A><BR>" ;
    else
```

Figure 62: GED2HTML - template file

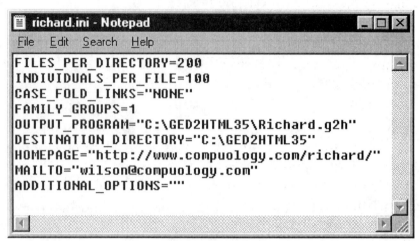

Figure 63: GED2HTML - options file

Once the template is set up the way you want the Web pages to look, save it with a name (such as *richard.g2h*). When you want to use those options in the future, you simply select that template.

This feature allows you to modify the headers or footers on the pages it creates. You can add such things as your e-mail address, Web page address, and even a copyright notice. Each HTML file can contain a single individual or multiple individuals. These files can be organized into subdirectories, or they can all be put into one main directory. It also allows for photos to be linked to the Web pages it creates.

This program is the most advanced of all of the shareware and freeware programs. It may be a little harder for the novice to use.

Installation procedure for GED2HTML:

1. Create a directory or folder where the program can be installed, i.e., **C:\GED2HTML** (For more on DOS commands, see "Basic DOS Commands" in *Appendix B*, starting on page 281.)

2. Unzip the file you downloaded and put the files it contains into the directory or folder you created. (For more information about unzip, see "Compression Programs" in *Appendix B*, starting on page 289).

3. Edit the template file *standard.g2h* (see Figure 62).

4. Create or edit the options file *filename.ini* (see Figure 63).

Once you have completed these steps, you run the program by typing GED2HTML from the DOS prompt (C:\). The "GEDCOM to HTML Translator" screen will appear (see Figure 64).

• Select the GEDCOM file you want to use to create the Web pages. If you do not know where your GEDCOM file is located, you can select the "Browse" button and locate the file on your hard drive.

• Next, select an option file, if you have created one. Otherwise, select the "Edit" button under the "Option Editing" area. You will then see the "Edit Options" screen (see Figure 65).

• Select a template file (if you have created one). Tell the program where to place the Web pages it creates (Target Directory), type in the location of your home page (Home page URL), and enter your e-mail address (Mailto address).

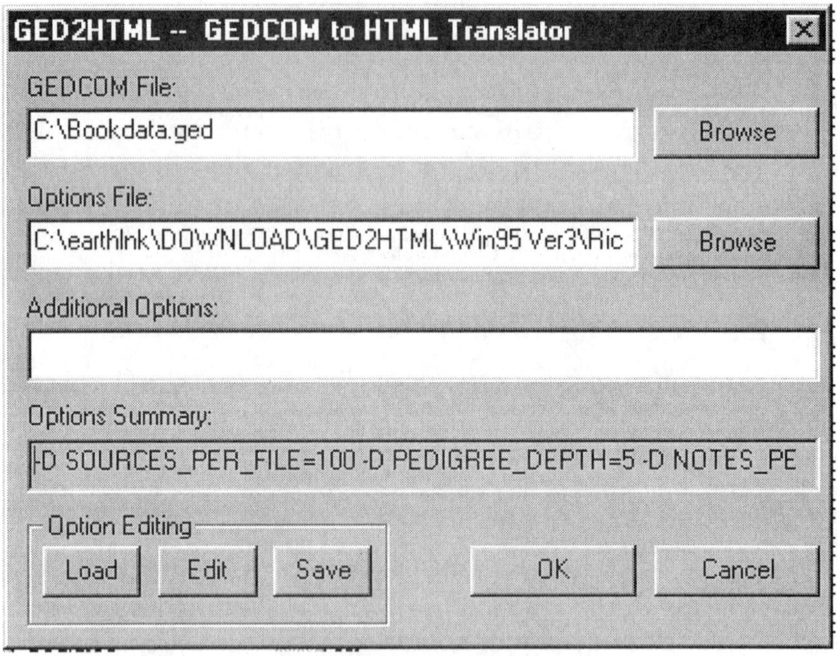

Figure 64: GED2HTML - main screen

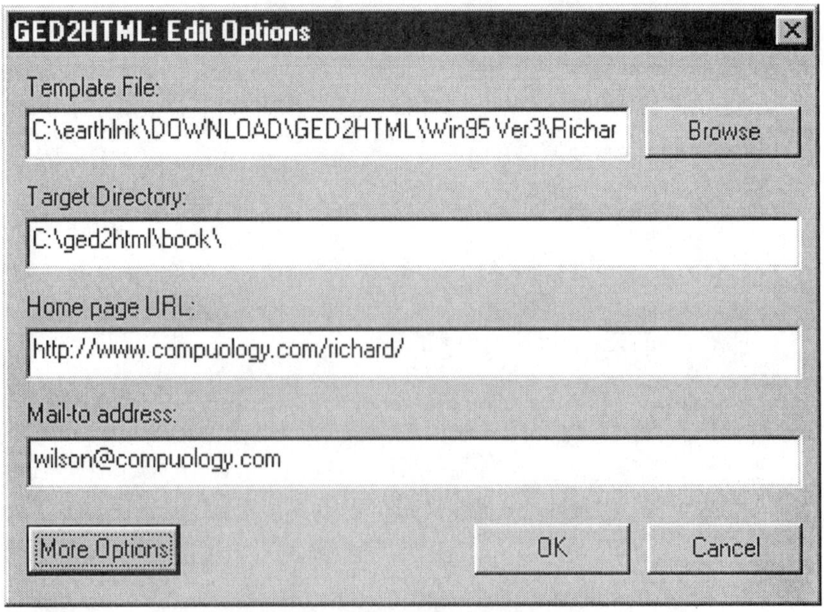

Figure 65: GED2HTML - Edit Options

- You can also select the "More Options" button and get another screen of options you can select (see Figure 66).

- You need to select the type of output you want: "Individuals" (see Figure 68) or "Family Group Sheet" (see Figure 69).

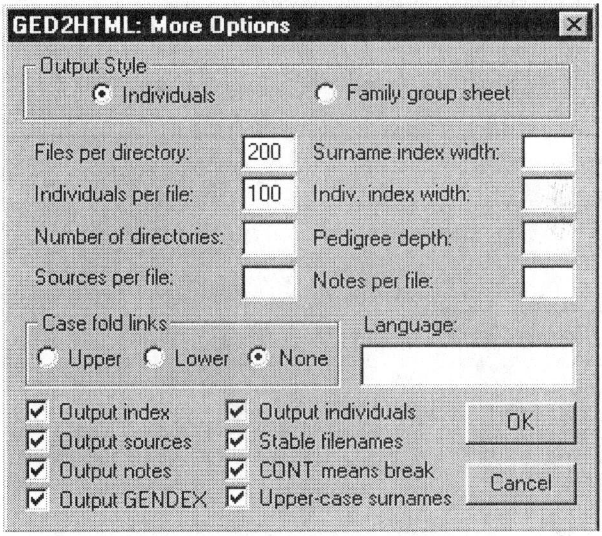

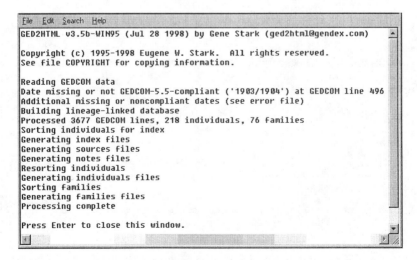

Figure 66: GED2HTML - More Options

Figure 67: GED2HTML - complete screen

- Once you have made all of your selections, you can save them for future use by selecting the "Save" button under the "Option Editing" (see Figure 64).

- Now that you have selected and saved all the options you want to use, select the "OK" button.

- The GED2HTML program then processes the Web pages. When complete, the program will give you a report of the work it has completed (see Figure 67).

Figures 68 and 69 show how the Web pages will look.

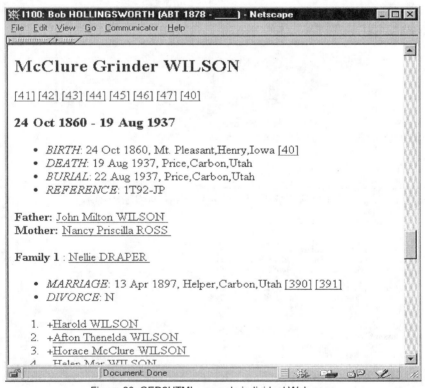

Figure 68: GED2HTML - sample individual Web page

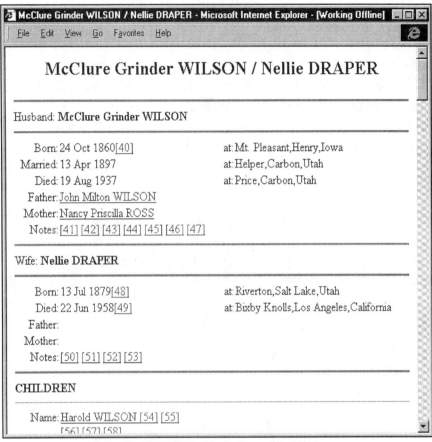

Figure 69: GED2HTML - Family Group Sheet Web page

GED2WWW

GED2WWW is a freeware GEDCOM-to-HTML conversion program that was written by Leslie Howard. The current version is 0.22, released on April 17, 1997. It creates HTML coded Web pages from a standard GEDCOM file. This program is available on the Internet at **http://pw2.netcom.com/~lhoward/ged2www.html**. The author can be contacted at *<lhoward@ix.netcom.com>*.

GED2WWW's features include:

- Minimal HTML coding (so the size of the files are small)
- Generates a text file suitable for indexing with Gendex
- Supports international characters
- Information of living people can be suppressed
- Summary, index, surname, and data pages
- Individuals dates (birth-death) can be listed on the index page
- User selectable text/background/link colors
- User selectable background images
- DOS and Unix versions available (it also runs under Windows or Win95/98)
- No cost (freeware)

It does not allow custom headers, photographs, special links, or footers for your copyright notice. All of these features would have to be manually added.

You need to understand some DOS commands to use this program (for more information on DOS see "Basic DOS Commands" in *Appendix B*, starting on page 281).

Here is the process of using the current version of GED2WWW.

1.   Create a folder (directory) for GED2WWW.

2.   Move the GED2WWW files to that folder—after extracting them from the ZIP archive (For more information about unziping files see "Compression Programs" in *Appendix B,* starting on page 289).

3.   Place the GEDCOM file you created into that same directory or folder.

4.   From the C:\GED2WWW prompt, type GED2WWW and the opening screen will appear (Figure 70). At the bottom of the screen, the program tells you that it will create a directory for your HTML files. Type the letter "Y" to continue.

GED2WWW version 0.22 (c) 1996, 1997 Leslie Howard.
Compiled Apr 17 1997 19:45:27.
GED2WWW is free software; you can redistribute it and/or modify it under the term of the GNU General Public License. This program is distributed in the hope that it will be useful, but WITHOUT ANY WARRANTY; without even the implied warranty of MERCHANTABILITY or FITNESS FOR A PARTICULAR PURPOSE. See the GNU General Public License for details.
A copy of the license can be found in the COPYING file.

GED2WWW converts GEDCOM files to HTML with an emphasis on producing as little HTML as possible without sacrificing vital content.

To learn more about GED2WWW visit the GED2WWW homepage at
http://www.netcom.com/~lhoward/ged2www.html
or email the author (Leslie Howard) at *<lhoward@ix.netcom.com>*
===
ATTENTION! GED2WWW needs to create a place to put the HTML files it produces. GED2WWW will create a directory called \html\ under the current directory. If this directory already exists, all HTML files in it will be deleted (such as the results from a previous GED2WWW database conversion).
Do you want to continue (Y/N) ?

Figure 70: GED2WWW - start up screen

5. The program will then ask you a series of questions about your database and how you want it set up. These questions are pretty self-explanatory. When it asks for the name of the GEDCOM file, you must include the *.ged* extension.

6. If you are making more than one set of HTML files to be accessed from your home page, make sure you put each set of HTML files in a separate subdirectory. Otherwise, the new Web pages will be copied over the old set of pages.

Sample Web pages created by the GED2WWW program can be seen in Figures 71, 72 and 73.

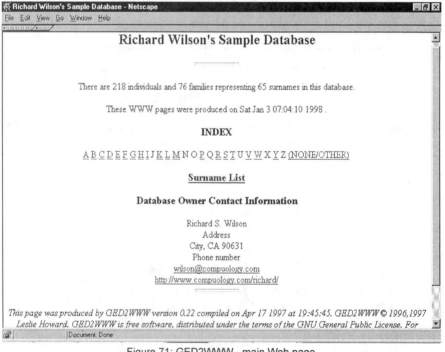

Figure 71: GED2WWW - main Web page

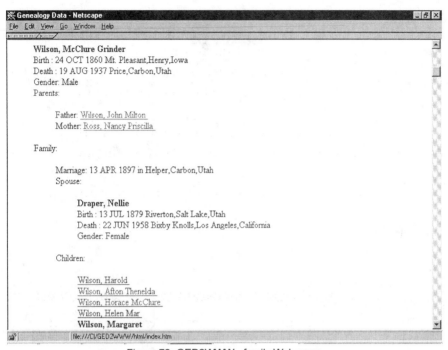

Figure 72: GED2WWW - family Web page

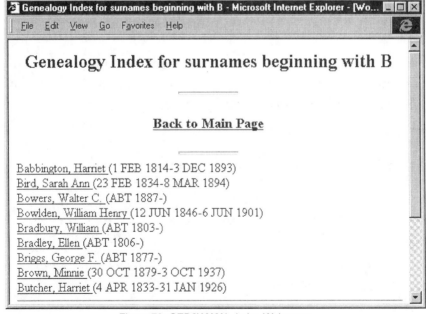

Figure 73: GED2WWW - index Web page

Gedpage

Gedpage is a GEDCOM-to-HTML conversion program available from the Web at **http://www.frontiernet.net/~rjacob/gedpage.htm** (there is also a Macintosh version available). Version 2.05 was created January 11, 1999. Gedpage is a shareware program with many of its features disabled until you pay the registration fee, which is only $10.00 and is good for ALL future versions. The author is currently working on Gedpage version 3, which will add even more features to this program.

This program creates Web pages in family group sheet format—familiar to most genealogists. It allows a link back to your home page. It also supports the GENDEX system. It includes optional notes, sources, and soundex codes (registered version only).

When you download this program from the Internet, it will be in the form of a self-extracting Zip file. It will unzip (expand) itself when you type the name of the file from the DOS prompt (C : \).

You need to understand some DOS commands to use this program (For more information on DOS commands see "Basic DOS Commands" in *Appendix B*, starting on page 281).

Here are the steps to install this program:

1. Change to the directory where you placed the file you downloaded (i.e., *gdpg202.exe*).

2. Type the name of the file (i.e., *gdpg202.exe*) and press **Enter** to unzip or expand it.

3. Type INSTALL to start the installation program. You will then see the dialog box in Figure 74. The program will be installed into the C:\GEDPAGE directory. If you wish to put it into another directory, simply type in the location.

4. Select the "Continue" button, the program installs itself and creates a Gedpage program group. It will then display a message indicating the installation is complete. Click on the "OK" button.

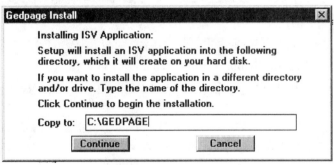

Figure 74: Gedpage - Install

The program is now installed on your computer and ready to be run. Before you run this program, however, you need to edit or delete the *header.htm* and the *footer.htm* files (see Figure 75). These files can be edited to include any text you want to appear on the header or footer of each Web page (such as the title of your genealogy Web page, copyright notices, etc.). If you delete or rename the files, you will have no message at all on the top and bottom of each Web page.

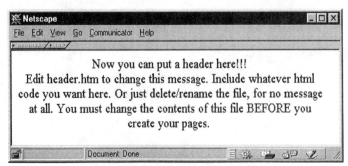

Figure 75: Gedpage - *header.htm* file

- To run the Gedpage program, simply click on the Gedpage 2.0 icon that was created in the Gedpage program group. The screen shown in Figure 76 will appear.

- Input the address of your home page URL, your e-mail address, and the location and name of the GEDCOM file you are using to create Web pages.

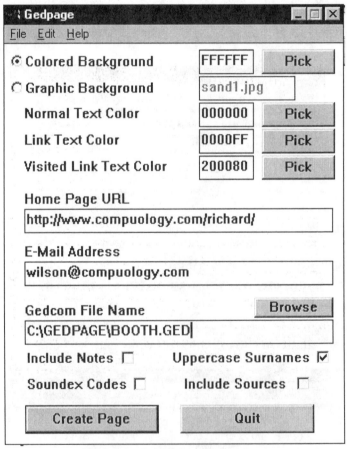

Figure 76: Gedpage - options screen

- It is very easy to select the various colors and backgrounds you want to use. Although the colors are shown with their number codes (i.e., 0000FF), when you click on the "Pick" button you will see the "Colors" screen in Figure 77. Once you select the desired color, its code is automatically inserted into the box on the main page (Figure 76).

- Click on the "Create Page" button. When the program is finished, a box appears saying it is done. Click on the "OK" button.

Colors		☒
White	Red	Green
Blue	Magenta	Cyan
Yellow	Black	Aquamarine
Blue Violet	Brown	Bronze
Copper	Dark Green	Dark Purple
Forest Green	Gold	Grey
Light Blue	Lime Green	Maroon
Midnight Blue	Neon Blue	Neon Pink
Orange	Pink	Scarlet
Silver	Sky Blue	Spicy Pink
Tan	Turquoise	Very Dark Brown
Violet	Violet Red	Off White

Figure 77: Gedpage - Colors

Figures 78 and 79 show two sample Web pages created by the Gedpage program.

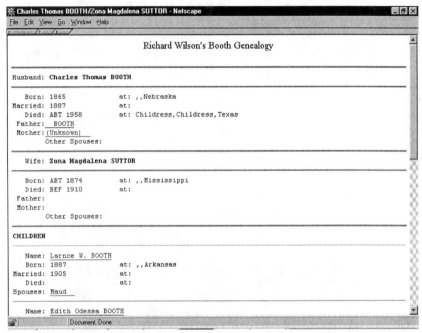

Figure 78: Gedpage - sample Web page

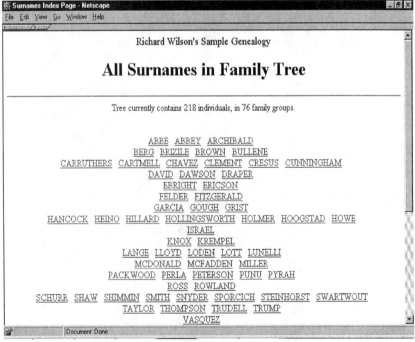

Figure 79: Gedpage - Surnames Index Page

Generations

Generations is a full-featured, commercial genealogy program. It is evolved from the Reunion program created by Leister Productions. Sierra Software produces the current version of the program, which is version 5.2 dated October 30, 1998. Their Internet Web site is located at: **http://www.sierra.com/sierrahome/familytree/**.

To create Web pages with this program:

1. Click on "Create" on the menu bar. Next, click on "Internet Family Tree . . ." from the pull-down menu that opens below "Create." The screen in Figure 80 will appear.

2. Select the "Format" you want: either "Internet Family Tree" or "Internet Family Tree and Person Sheets." For an example of a Person Sheet see Figure 88.

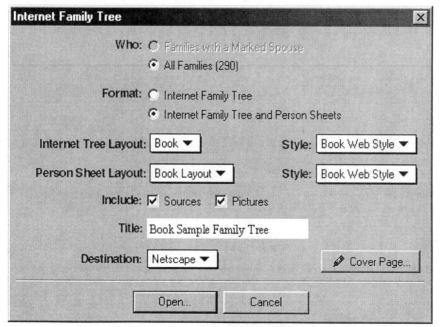

Figure 80: Generations - Internet Family Tree

3.   Select "Define Layouts . . ." from the Internet Tree Layout or the Person Sheet Layout drop-down menu. The "Internet Family Tree Layout" screen in Figure 81 will appear.

4.   Place an "X" in each of the information fields you want included for the individuals on your Web pages. Once you have made all your selections, click on the "Save" button.

5.   Select "Define Styles . . ." from the Internet Tree Style or the Person Sheet Style drop-down menu. The "Define HTML Style" screen in Figure 82 will appear.

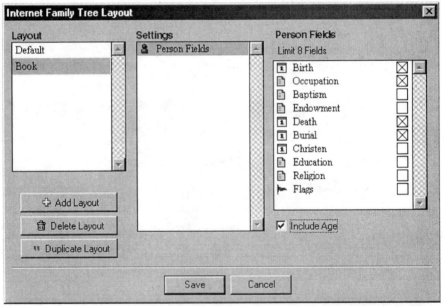

Figure 81: Generations - Internet Family Tree Layout

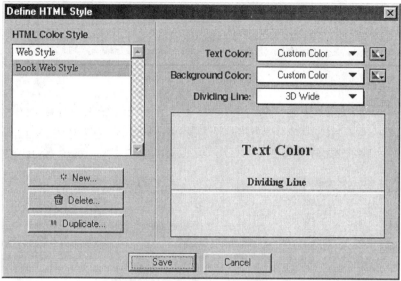

Figure 82: Generations - Define HTML Style

6. Select the colors and line styles for your Web pages using the pull-down bars. If you select "Custom Color," the colored square to the right of the bars appears for you to select a custom color. Once you have made all of your selections, click on the "Save" button.

7. Click on the "Cover Page . . ." button to create a main Web page (see Figure 83).

8. Click on the "Graphic" pull-down bar to select a graphic to be displayed on the cover page.

9. Select the style of the Web page and the text colors of the page with the other pull-down bars. The introductory text can be typed in the "Intro" box, or you can click on the "Import" button to bring in a text file you already have saved on your computer.

10. Fill in the contact information and then click on the "Save button.

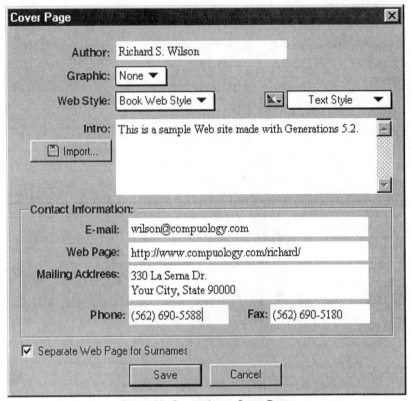

Figure 83: Generations - Cover Page

11. Once you have made all of your selections, click on the "Open. . ." button to save your Web pages. The "Save Web File" dialog box will appear (see Figure 84).

12. Input the name of the folder where you want the Web pages to be created (or accept the default folder). Click on the "Save" button and the Web pages will be saved at the location you specified. The main Web page then opens in your Web browser (see Figure 85).

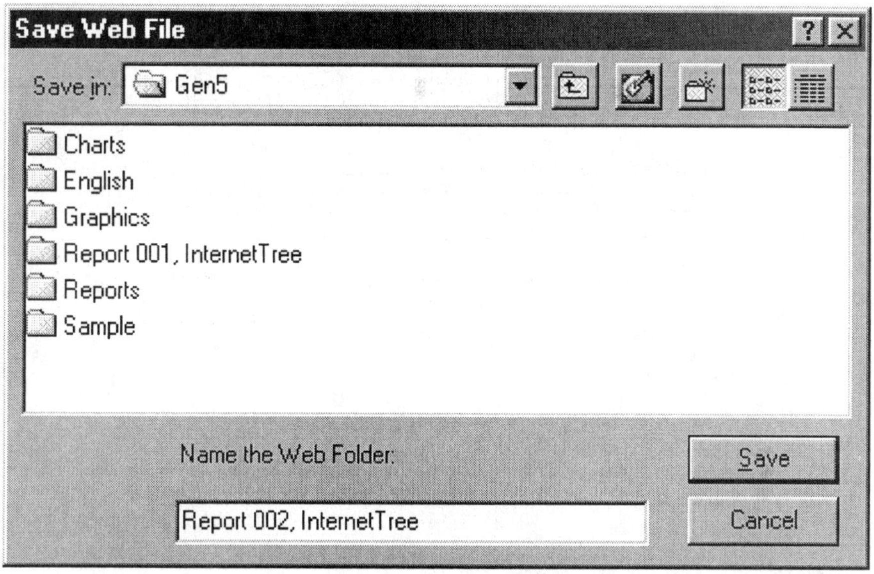

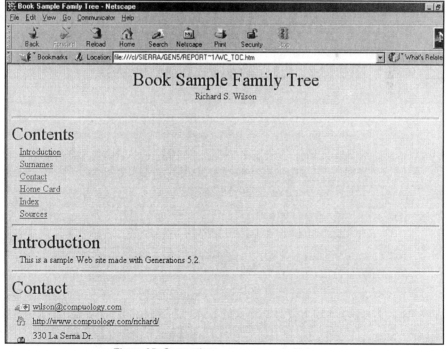

Figure 84: Generations - Save Web File

Figure 85: Generations - cover page in Netscape

Figures 85 through 88 show examples of a few Web pages created with the Generations program.

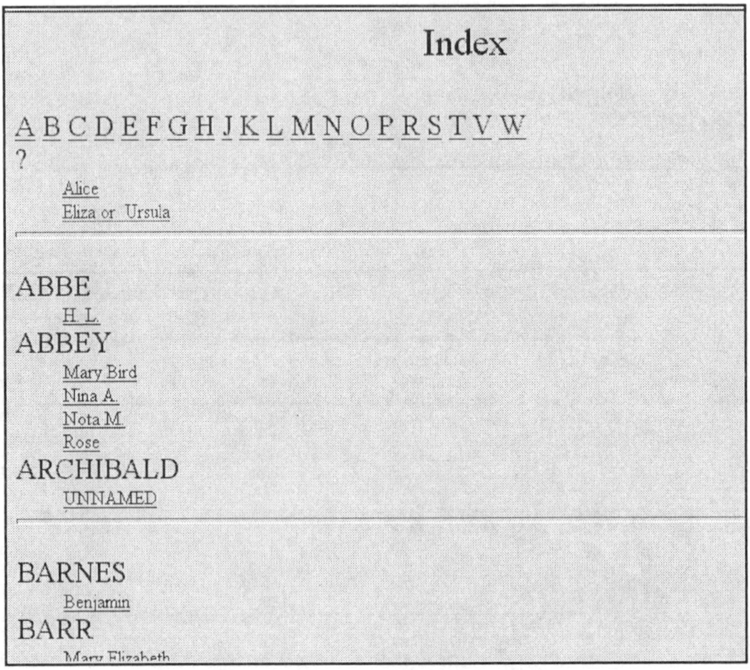

Figure 86: Generations - sample index Web page

The small camera icon on the Family Web Page (Figure 87) allows you to view the images you included on your Web page (if you selected the "Pictures" box on the Internet Family Tree screen as seen in Figure 80–assuming you had any photos linked to your selected records). To view the photos, click on the camera icon.

Not only can Generations create Internet Family Tree style Web pages, but also Web pages from most of their standard reports (such as a family group sheet or pedigree Web page). To generate these types of Web pages, proceed as if you were going to create one of these standard reports, then simply select Web Folder from the choices provided in the "Destination:" pull-down menu.

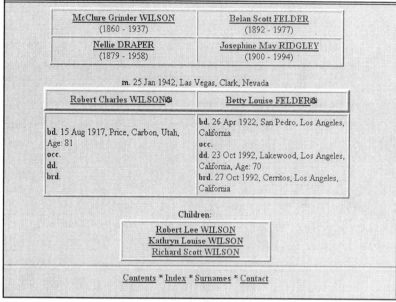

McClure Grinder WILSON (1860 - 1937)	Belan Scott FELDER (1892 - 1977)
Nellie DRAPER (1879 - 1958)	Josephine May RIDGLEY (1900 - 1994)

m. 25 Jan 1942, Las Vegas, Clark, Nevada

Robert Charles WILSON☺	Betty Louise FELDER☺
bd. 15 Aug 1917, Price, Carbon, Utah, Age: 81 occ. dd. brd.	bd. 26 Apr 1922, San Pedro, Los Angeles, California occ. dd. 23 Oct 1992, Lakewood, Los Angeles, California, Age: 70 brd. 27 Oct 1992, Cerritos, Los Angeles, California

Children:

Robert Lee WILSON
Kathryn Louise WILSON
Richard Scott WILSON

Contents * Index * Surnames * Contact

Figure 87: Generations - family Web page sample

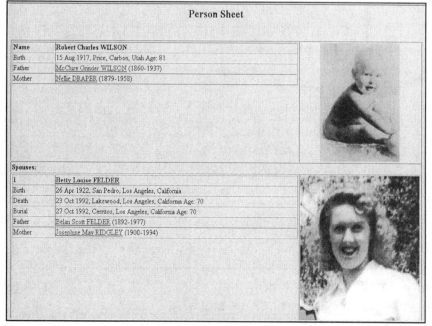

Person Sheet

Name	Robert Charles WILSON
Birth	15 Aug 1917, Price, Carbon, Utah Age: 81
Father	McClure Grinder WILSON (1860-1937)
Mother	Nellie DRAPER (1879-1958)

Spouses:	
1	Betty Louise FELDER
Birth	26 Apr 1922, San Pedro, Los Angeles, California
Death	23 Oct 1992, Lakewood, Los Angeles, California Age: 70
Burial	27 Oct 1992, Cerritos, Los Angeles, California Age: 70
Father	Belan Scott FELDER (1892-1977)
Mother	Josephine May RIDGLEY (1900-1994)

Figure 88: Generations: - Person Sheet

Legacy

Legacy is a full-featured, commercial genealogy software program. You will be able to create a wide variety of Web pages that are good looking, as well as functional. This program will automatically include photographs and sounds you have entered into the program. It can suppress information about living people, create a Gendex file, link a GEDCOM file, and include links to your home page and e-mail address.

The latest version of the program is 2.0, dated April 14, 1999. However, they are constantly updating this program, so the build date changes every few weeks. Web page creation is new and only available in this version of Legacy. To update to the version with the Web page feature, check for the update at the **http://www.legacyfamilytree.com/** site.

To create Web pages:

1.   From the "Eile" pull-down menu, select "Create Web Pages..." Once the program starts, you will see the "Web Page Creation" screen shown in Figure 89.

2.   Select all the options you want by clicking on the various tabs. These include the title of your page and project (which is also where it stores the finished Web pages), the name and address you want to appear on the Web pages, an introductory paragraph, and your e-mail address.

3.   On the right side of the screen, in the "Web Page Style" section, you can choose one of four styles for your Web pages.

4.   From the "Who to Include" tab, choose which people's data you want to include on your Web pages (see Figure 90).

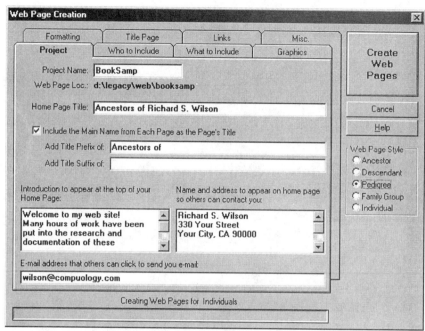

Figure 89: Legacy - Web Page Creation

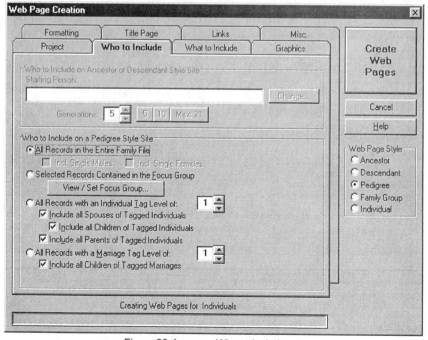

Figure 90: Legacy - Who to Include tab

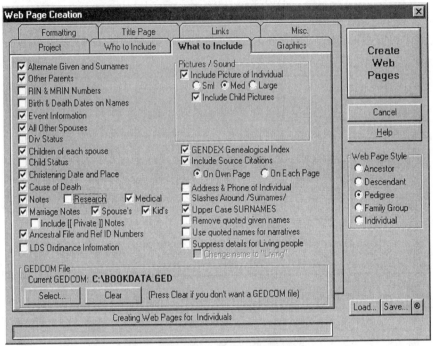

Figure 91: Legacy - What to Include tab

5. From the "What to Include" tab, select all of the important details you want on your Web pages. These include such items as pictures, notes, names Gendex file, GEDCOM file, and whether to include details for living people (see figure 91).

6. From the "Graphics" tab, select the graphics you want to use on your Web pages. You can select a background image, as well as the types of arrows and bullets to use (see Figure 92).

7. From the "Formatting" tab, format how the names and headers will be laid out (see Figure 93). You can also decide what style you want the text of the Web pages to be in, either list type or narrative (book style).

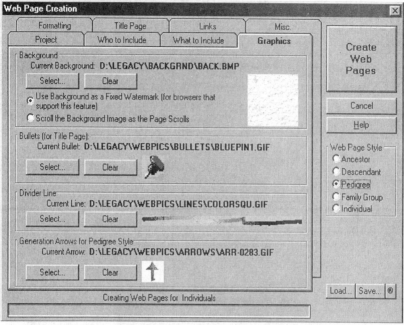

Figure 92: Legacy - Graphics tab

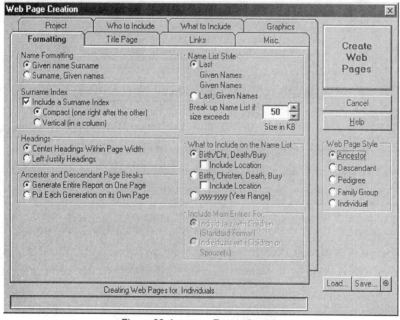

Figure 93: Legacy - Formatting tab

8. From the "Title Page" tab, input the name of the graphic you would like to appear on the main Web page.

9. From the "Links" tab, you can add a link back to your main Web home page from one or all the Web pages you create. You can also easily add custom headers and footers to every Web page you create (see Figure 94).

10. From the "Misc." tab, you are able to input both a Web site description and a keyword list that will be put into meta tags (see Figure 95). This will enable your Web pages to be listed near the top of a search engine list (see "Meta Tags" in *Chapter 5*, starting on page 170).

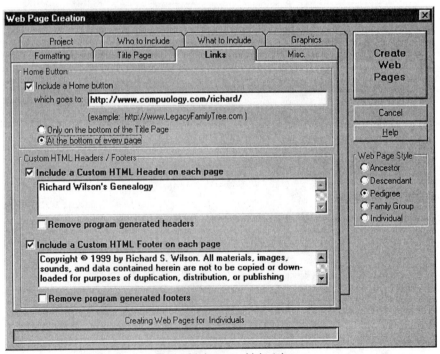

Figure 94: Legacy - Links tab

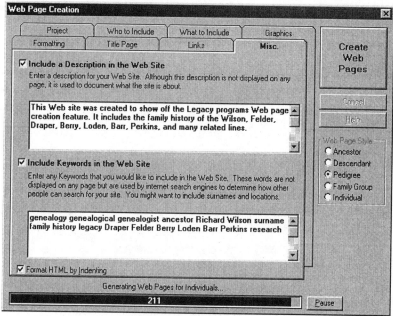
Figure 95: Legacy - Misc. tab

11. Once you have finished selecting all of the options you desire, you simply select the "Create Web Pages" button. When the program has completed its processing, you will see a box indicating the creation is complete. Select the "OK" button.

Legacy will create many different types of Web page outputs, including birthday and anniversary pages. Figures 96 through 99 show several samples of different Web pages created by this program.

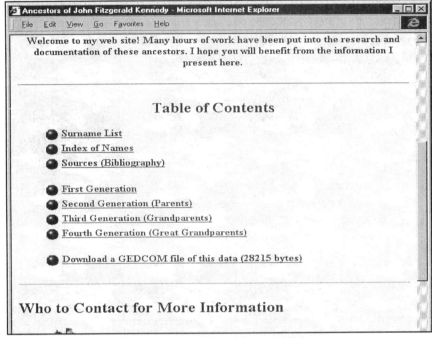

Figure 96: Legacy - Table of Contents Web page

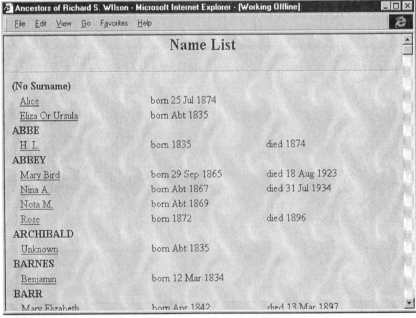

Figure 97: Legacy - Name List Web page

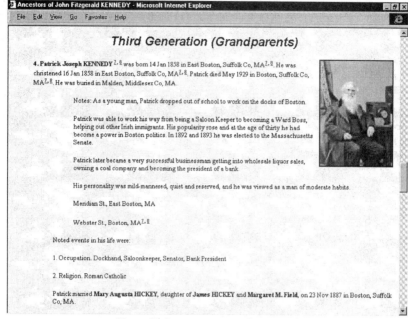

Figure 98: Legacy - ancestor Web page

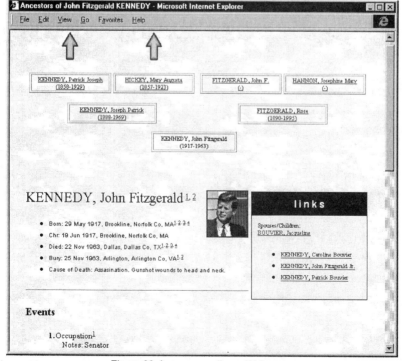

Figure 99: Legacy - pedigree Web page

The Master Genealogist

The Master Genealogist is a full-featured, commercial genealogy program created by Wholly Genes software. The current version is 3.7, dated December 13, 1998. Their Web site is located at: **http://www.whollygenes.com/**.

The Master Genealogist creates a GENDEX file and Web pages in many different formats. Some of these are:
- Genealogy (Register) Report
- Descendancy Narrative
- Descendancy Charts
- Table of Contents
- End Notes
- Biography
- Indexes (lists of names, places, and marriages)

Creating Web pages with The Master Genealogist is a two-step process. First you create a custom report for the type of Web pages you want to generate, then you actually use the report to create the Web pages.

To create a report-style Web page with this program:

1. Click on "Report" on the menu bar. Next, click on "Custom Report Writer . . ." from the pull-down menu that opens below Report. The screen in Figure 100 appears.

2. Click on the Wizard button and the "TMG Report Wizard" screen opens (see Figure 101).

3. Select (highlight) the type of Web page you want to create and click on the "Next ->" button.

4. A screen appears that asks you which records you want to include in the report. After you have chosen, click on the "<u>N</u>ext ->" button.

5. The next screen gives you one or more style layouts to use. After you have chosen, click on the "<u>N</u>ext ->" button.

6. From the "Destination" screen (see Figure 102), click on the "File" button.

7. Select "Hypertext Markup Lang (HTML)" from the list in the window at the bottom of the screen (see Figure 102), then click on the "<u>N</u>ext ->" button.

8. The next screen asks about page numbering. Select "None" and then click on the "<u>N</u>ext ->" button.

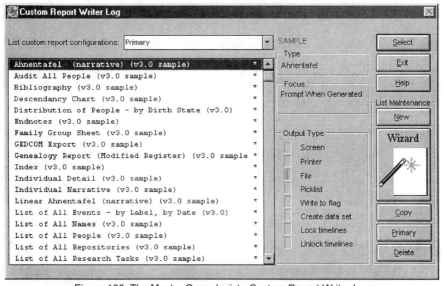

Figure 100: The Master Genealogist - Custom Report Writer Log

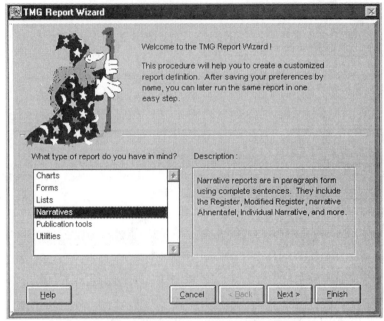

Figure 101: The Master Genealogist - Report Wizard

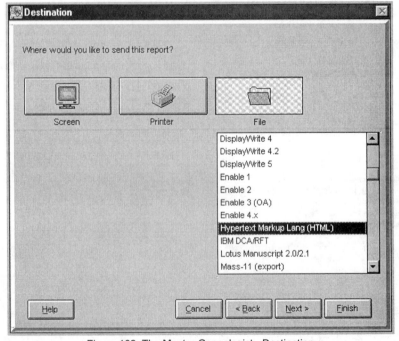

Figure 102: The Master Genealogist - Destination

9. The next few screens ask you to make decisions about whether or not to include memos, source citations, indexes, table of contents, and bibliography in your report. Select your options and click on the "N̲ext ->" button on each screen.

10. From the "Last Step" screen (see Figure 103), enter the name you want to use to describe your new report. Click on the "F̲inish" button and you will be taken back to the Custom Report Writer screen (Figure 100).

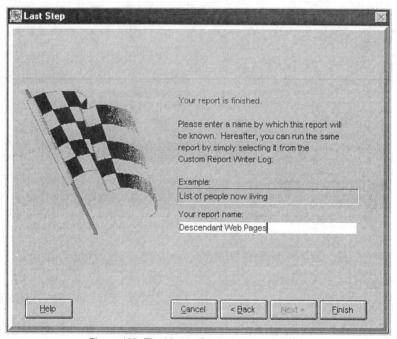

Figure 103: The Master Genealogist - Last Step

To generate your Web pages:

1. From the screen in Figure 100, highlight the name of the new report you just created and click on the "S̲elect" button (you can also use any samples provided or reports you previously designed and saved). You then see the "Report Definition" screen in Figure 104.

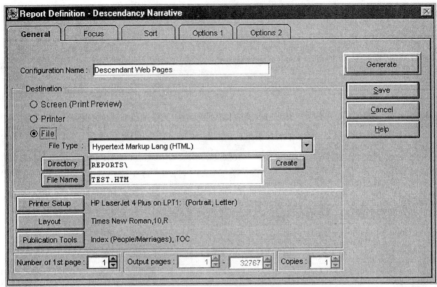

Figure 104: The Master Genealogist - Report Definition

2. Choose a file name of five characters or less (if you use more than five characters, TMG will truncate the trailing characters and substitute three characters that are unique for each file). Type the filename to the right of the "File Name" button.

3. Make sure the destination selected is "File" and the "File Type:" is Hypertext Markup Lang (HTML). If it is not, click on the arrow button to the right of the field and highlight it from the pull-down menu.

4. Click on the "Focus" tab to select which records you want to include on your Web pages.

5. Click on the "Options 1" and "Options 2" tabs to select which data to include on your Web pages. From the "Options 1" tab you can suppress data for living individuals (see Figure 105).

6. To include images on your pages, click on the "Publication Tools" button from the General tab. The "Publication Tools" screen will appear.

7. Click on the "Exhibits" tab and you will see the options for embedding your images (see Figure 106). Do not check the "Reference full path names" box or the Web page link will try to find the images on your hard drive. Click on the OK button to go back to the "Report Definition" screen.

> The Master Genealogist includes photos on Web pages in the same format as they were imported in. Only JPG and GIF images can be viewed by most Web browsers. If your images were stored in PCX or other formats, they will appear as broken images on your Web pages.

8. After you have selected all the options you want on your Web pages, click on the "Generate" button. You will get a warning screen telling you the filename has been changed. Click the "OK" button and the "Document Summary Screen" appears (see Figure 107).

9. From the "Document Summary Screen," you see the descriptive phrases that will be hidden on your Web page as meta tags. Be sure to include your keywords here. (See "Meta Tags" in *Chapter 5*, starting on page 170). Click on the "OK" button and your Web pages are processed. The "HTML File List" screen appears to show you the file names that were produced (see Figure 108).

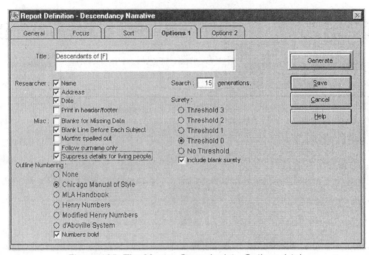

Figure 105: The Master Genealogist - Options 1 tab

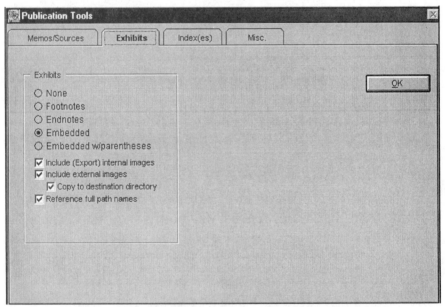

Figure 106: The Master Genealogist - Publication Tools

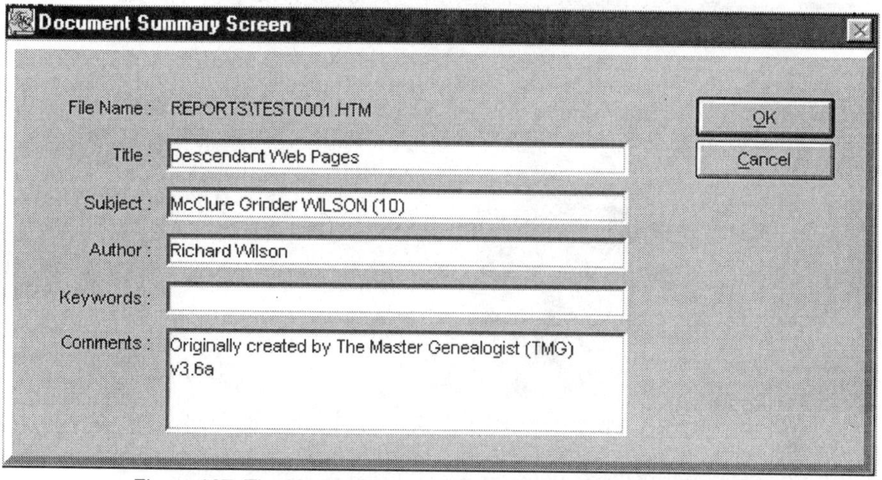

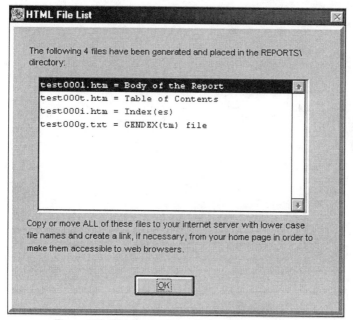

Figure 107: The Master Genealogist - Document Summary Screen

Figure 108: The Master Genealogist - HTML File List

Figures 109 and 110 are samples of Web pages created with The Master Genealogist.

Descendants of McClure Grinder Wilson

Generation One

1. McClure Grinder[1] WILSON;   and Nellie Draper. McClure was born 24 Oct 1860 at Mt. Pleasant, Henry, Iowa;[1] married Ann Hillard circa 1886 at Mt. Pleasnt, Henry, Iowa;[2] married Nellie Draper 13 Apr 1897 at Helper, Carbon, Utah;[3,4] died 19 Aug 1937 at Price, Carbon, Utah, at age 76; buried 22 Aug 1937 at Price, Carbon, Utah.

Children of McClure Grinder[1] Wilson and Nellie Draper all born at Price, Carbon, Utah, were as follows:

- + 2 i. Harold[2] WILSON, divorced Mary Cartmell; born 5 Aug 1898; marriedMary Cartmell; married Thelma Rose McDonald.
- + 3 ii. Afton Thenelda WILSON, born 13 Sep 1900; married Henry George Cunningham.
- + 4 iii. Horace McClure WILSON, divorced Evelyn Berg; born 5 Sep 1902; married Evelyn Berg.
- 5 iv. Helen Mar WILSON and Paul W. Krempel were divorced; born 15 Jul 1906;[5] married Paul W. Krempel 9 Apr

Figure 109: The Master Genealogist - Descendants Web page

Index of People

(--?--)
    (--?--) (b. circa 1953)
    (--?--) (b. circa 1953)
    Linda (b. circa 1953)
    Linda (b. circa 1953)
Berg
    Evelyn (b. 03 Jun 1908, d. Dec 1991)
    Evelyn (b. 03 Jun 1908, d. Dec 1991)
    Evelyn (b. 03 Jun 1908, d. Dec 1991)
    Evelyn (b. 03 Jun 1908, d. Dec 1991)
Carruthers
    Annett Jean (b. 17 Apr 1949)
    Charles Allen (b. 27 Aug 1927)
    Charles Allen (b. 27 Aug 1927)
    Clyde Austin (b. 08 Feb 1888)
    Clyde Austin (b. 08 Feb 1888)
    Donald Austin (b. 04 Jun 1921)
    Donald Austin (b. 04 Jun 1921)
    Geraldine Lee (b. 31 May 1951)
    June Marie (b. 04 Jun 1915)
    June Marie (b. 04 Jun 1915)
    Mabel (b. 04 Oct 1890)
    Olive Bernece (b. 04 Aug 1917)
    Olive Bernece (b. 04 Aug 1917)
    Samuel McClure (b. 21 Aug 1913, d. 10 Nov 1946)

Figure 110: The Master Genealogist - Index of People

Ultimate Family Tree

The Ultimate Family Tree is a full-featured, commercial genealogy program. It was created by Palladium Software to replace Roots V and Family Gathering (both of these programs also had the ability to create Web pages). The current version of the program is 2.9, dated September 8, 1998. Their Web site is at: **http://www.uftree.com/**.

Ultimate Family Tree creates a main Web page with the project information, links to the various generation charts, and a surname listing of every surname in the database. It also includes Web pages for all the family members who were in the database (see Figure 116). It creates a nice looking surname index page, which includes birth and death dates for each individual (see Figure 117). This program does not have the option of making custom headers and footers, however.

To create Web pages with this program:

•   Click on the "Online" button on the menu bar. Click on "Instant Web Page" from the pull-down menu. You will see the "Instant Web Page" screen in Figure 111.

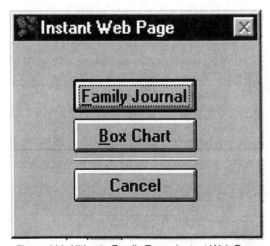

Figure 111: Ultimate Family Tree - Instant Web Page

- You can choose between two types of Web pages. "Family Journal" will give you a set of narrative (book style) Web pages (see Figure 116). "Box Chart" creates Web pages made up of descending box charts (see Figure 118).

- Click on the "Family Journal" button and the "Instant Web Page" options screen appears (see Figure 112).

- Select the type of Web pages you want to create, either descendant (from an ancestor down to his descendants) or Reverse Register (from a person back to their ancestors). You can also select the items you want to include on your Web pages by placing a check mark in the appropriate boxes. This program also has the option of removing information about living people.

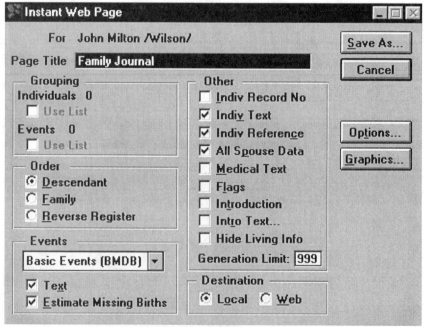

Figure 112: Ultimate Family Tree - Instant Web Page

- Click on the "Options" button and the "Instant Web Page Options" screen appears (see Figure 113).

- Select which images you want to include on your Web pages, add your e-mail and an FTP address for your GEDCOM file (it you want to make it available online). There are also some additional options for configuring your data. Click on the "OK" button and you will go back to the screen in Figure 112.

- Click on the "Graphics" button and the "Instant Web Page Graphics" screen appears (see Figure 114). Here you have the ability to set up which graphics and sounds are used on your Web pages. Click on the "OK" button and you will go back to the screen in Figure 112.

- Once you have chosen all the options and features you want to include on your Web pages, you click on the "Save As" button. You will then be asked to give the Web pages a name (see Figure 115).

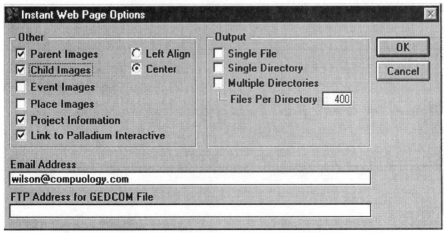

Figure 113: Ultimate Family Tree - Instant Web Page Options

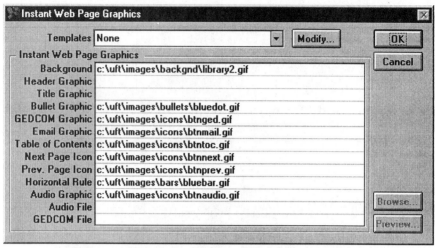

Figure 114: Ultimate Family Tree - Instant Web Page Graphics

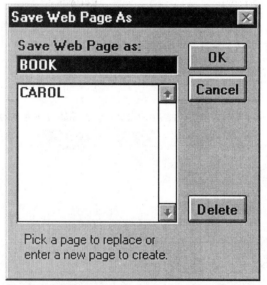

Figure 115: Ultimate Family Tree - Save Web Page As

- Click on the "OK" button and the program will create the Web pages. The pages will be stored in the project name directory, under the HTML directory. The above project (book) will be saved in **c:\uft\html\book**.

Figures 116 through 119 are samples of Web pages created by the Ultimate Family Tree program.

Figure 116: Ultimate Family Tree - Family information page

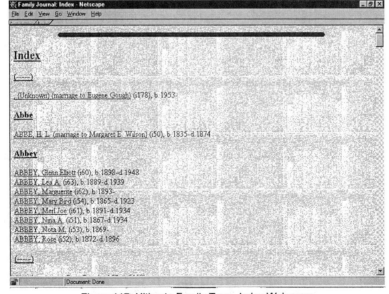

Figure 117: Ultimate Family Tree - Index Web page

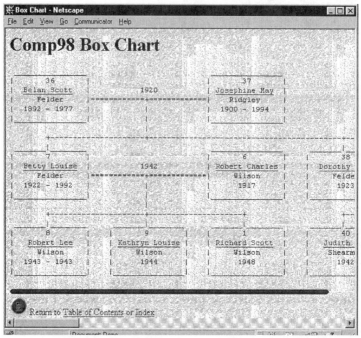

Figure 118: Ultimate Family Tree - Box Chart Web page

Figure 119: Ultimate Family Tree - Descendant List Web page

Webbit

Webbit (**http://www.compuology.com/genfiles/webbit14.zip**) is a GEDCOM-to-HTML conversion program. The current version is 1.4, dated January 5, 1997. The program's author is John Hemsley. It is a set of freeware programs which will convert GEDCOM files into hypertext pages you can put on your Web site. This program makes a wide variety of Web pages that are very unique.

You should be aware that Webbit has the following limitations:

20 children per family

5 marriages per person

5 entries per year on the timeline

5 generations on the descendants page

9,999 individuals per GEDCOM file

9,999 families per GEDCOM file

As you can see, Webbit is not suitable for a very large database, although you can still use it if you separate your large database into smaller databases.

Another limitation you should be aware of is that this program does not have options for custom headers and footers. If you have some knowledge of the Basic programming language, you can edit the *filename.bas* files to add text (see the custom footer on the bottom of the Web page in Figure 121).

You will need to know a few DOS commands to install and use this program (see the "Basic DOS Commands" section of *Appendix B*, starting on page 281).

Here is the installation procedure for Webbit:

1. Create a directory or folder to install the program into (i.e., **C:\WEBBIT**).

2. Unzip the *webbit14.zip* file and put the files it contains into the directory or folder you created. (For more information about unzipping files see "Compression Programs" in *Appendix B*, starting on page 289).

3. Create a directory off the Webbit directory named **DATA**.

4. Create a directory off the Webbit directory named **TEMP**.

5. Create a folder or directory off the Webbit directory with the name of the GEDCOM file you are converting.

6. Move the file *webbit.fot* into the data subdirectory.

7. Copy your GEDCOM file (with the same name as in step 4) to the **C:\WEBBIT\DATA** directory.

```
C:\webbit\webbit1.bat

Before you run this batch file make sure that you have created
subdirectories DATA and TEMP under the directory WEBBIT
Also make sure that your GED file has been copied to the WEBBIT\DATA
directory
Enter the name of your GEDCOM file below (max. 8 characters)
The name of the Gedcom File is : book.ged

 If you wish you can enter a 1 character prefix for your family files :
Type a prefix (A to Z) or press enter :
```

Figure 120: Webbit - step one

To create Web pages with Webbit:

- From the C:\Webbit\> prompt, type *webbit1.bat* and press <ENTER>. This will start the program.

- It will ask you if you want to add a letter before each of the files it creates (see Figure 120). This is necessary if you are putting more than one family's Web pages in the same directory.

- Next, type *webbit2* at the C:\webbit> prompt and press ENTER. This runs a series of programs which will convert the family history details, extracted by the first program, into a number of HTML files (*.HTM).

Once the program is complete, you will have Web pages suitable for use on the Web. Webbit makes some very unusual and creative pages.

Here is a list of the types of Web pages it creates:

1. A Web page for each family (files named *fxxx.htm*) that shows the four (4) grand-parents (where known), the parents and the children. (See Figure 121.)

2. Each family with children has a descendant Web page created (files named *dxxxx.htm*). If you do not want these pages to be created you can suppressed them using the setup options in the *option.ini* file.

3. A birth line Web page that indicates who was born in each year (a file named *timeb.htm*).

4. A Web page for each photograph listed in the *webbit.fot* file (files named *ixxxxxx.htm*). This file has to be created manually (with a text editor or word processor).

5. A photo index Web page for each person listed in the *webbit.fot* file (files named *pxxxx.htm*).

6. A name list Web page showing all of the people in your GEDCOM file. (A file named *namex.htm*).

7. A month-by-month anniversary list Web page showing which major events took place in each month—birthdays, deaths, and weddings (a file named *annvrs.htm*). (See Figure 122.)

8. An information Web page showing when, how, and by whom the GEDCOM file was created, plus some vital statistics about the data on the Web pages (a file named *info.htm*).

A Web page is also created for the notes of each family. This lists each person in the family with the events in their life. Events shown include the birth, christening, marriages, divorces, death, and burial, as well as address and occupation information. You also have the option to show any notes or sources alongside the event (files named *nxxxx.htm*). These pages may be suppressed by changing the *option.ini* file.

Webbit also creates a *Gendex.gdx* file from your GEDCOM file which contains the information needed by Gendex. This file is stored in the family subdirectory.

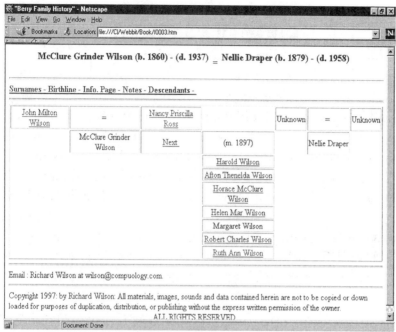

Figure 121: Webbit - family group Web page

Anniversaries

Jan- Feb- Mar- Apr- May- Jun- Jul- Aug- Sep- Oct- Nov- Dec

Surnames - Birthline - Info. Page -

Jan	----------First Person----------	---------Second Person--------	-----Date-----	No. of Years
Birthday	Robert Lee Wilson		4 JAN 1943	54
Birthday	Margaret Wilson		25 JAN 1912	85
Birthday	Alfred Wilson		13 JAN 1892	105
Birthday	John McClure Wilson		14 JAN 1939	58
Birthday	Merl Joe Abbey		12 JAN 1891	106
Birthday	Ruby Knox		9 JAN 1974	23
Birthday	Raymond Garcia		7 JAN 1959	38
Death	Margaret Wilson		25 JAN 1912	85
Death	John Milton Wilson		11 JAN 1884	113
Death	Ross Wilson		30 JAN 1902	95
Marriage	Robert Charles Wilson	Betty Louise Felder	25 JAN 1942	55
Marriage	Clyde Austin Carruthers	Mabel Wilson	12 JAN 1912	85
Marriage	Saul Miller	Olive Wilson	14 JAN 1864	133
Go to Top				

Figure 122: Webbit - Anniversaries Web page

Conversion Summary

Just like choosing your main genealogy program, choosing a conversion program depends on what you would like the program to accomplish. Check out the Web pages of the various programs you are interested in using. Try out a few of them and see how well they work for you.

The following two charts show a comparison of several features of these programs. I used a GEDCOM file (95kb), with 218 people and 76 marriages for the conversion process of each program.

Program name	Web Pages	Total Size	Graphics	Graphics Size
Ancestral Quest	13	45.4kb	8	3.28meg
Family Origins	68	110kb	14	274kb
Family Tree Maker	n/	n/a	n/a	n/a
GED2HTM	2	85.2kb	n/a	n/a
GED2HTML	10	959.3k	n/a	n/a
GED2WWW	26	96kb	n/a	n/a
GEDPage	78	201kb	n/a	n/a
Generations	21	80kb	7	226kb
Legacy	22	1.27M	7	204kb
The Master Genealogist	4	118kb	4	2.21Meg
Ultimate Family Tree	57	158kb	12	36.5 kb
Webbit	24	591kb	n/a	n/a

Figure 123: Web Pages Creation Results Chart

Program name	Ancestral Quest	Family Origins	Family Tree Maker	GED2HTM	GED2HTML	GED2WWW	GEDPage	Generations	Legacy	The Master Genealogist	Ultimate Family Tree	Webbit
Hides living information	●					●			●	●	●	
Includes your name & address	●	●	●			●		●	●	●	●	
Includes your e-mail address	●	●	●		●	●	●	●	●	●	●	
Link to your home page URL	●		●		●	●	●	●	●			
Includes notes	●	●	●		●		●	●	●	●	●	●
Link to a GEDCOM file	●	●							●		●	
Creates GENDEX file					●	●	●		●	●		●
Custom headers/footers	●			●	●		●		●			
Creates pedigree charts	●		▼	●	●			●	●	●		
Creates family group charts	●		▼		●	●	●	●	●	●		●
Book format (ancestors)	●	●	▼					●	●	●	●	
Book format (descendants)	●	●	▼					●	●	●	●	
Creates surname index	●	●			●	●	●	●	●	●	●	
Creates name index	●	●			●	●		●	●	●	●	●
Creates anniversary list									●			●
Puts photos on some pages	●	●			▼			●	●	●	●	▼
Additional photos on pages	●							●	●	●	●	

Legend: [blank] = *No,* ● = *Yes,* ▼ = *Limited*
Figure 124: Conversion Program Feature Comparison Chart

Putting
it all
Together

## Chapter 5

Creating Your Web Pages

Now that you know a little bit about what Web pages are made of, you are ready to create your own home page. The two essential pieces of software required to create Web pages are a text editor (word processor or HTML editor) and a Web browser.

Keep in mind that Web pages are nothing more than files you create and save on your hard drive and later upload to a Web server (a host computer permanently connected to the Internet). These files you create are coded with special HTML codes using your text editor. These codes tell Web browsers how to display the Web pages. Be aware that a single Web page (one file) may appear to be many screens long when viewed with a Web browser or printed out on paper.

As you develop your Web pages, keep in mind a few principles for creating a well-designed Web site. Good design and focused content are essential to creating a successful site that grabs and keeps the attention of your visitors. A good site has a constantly increasing number of accesses (visits) as news is spread by word of mouth and links to it are created.

The following guidelines should be applied to all your Web pages:

1. Keep your pages short, no more than two or three screens long at the most (larger pages will take too long to load).

2. Introduce pages with a short description of their contents, and then links to related materials.

3. Individual sections of text should be kept short.

4. Each page should be self-explanatory. Understanding the content of a page should not depend on a reader having arrived at it from another page (they may find one of your pages with a search engine.)

5. Your pages need to communicate information in a clear, succinct, and specific way.

6. Graphics should be used to enhance your page, but try not to overwhelm the visitor with a large number of graphics (nobody wants to wait 20 minutes for one page to load–which will happen if you include too many graphics on your Web page).

Keeping these guidelines in mind, start designing your main Web page. This is the one that has links to your converted genealogy Web pages. This is also the first page people will see when they visit your Web site.

Home pages (your main Web page) are usually named *index.html* or *index.htm*. Therefore, if the Web address your Internet Service Provider gave you was **http://www.provider.com/~yourname**, then the complete address of your home page (main page) would probably be **http://www.provider.com/~yourname/index.html**.

As long as the name of your main Web page is *index.htm* or *index.html,* then the only part of your Web address someone has to type to find your site is **http://www.yourprovider.com/~yourname/**. This is because Web browsers look for standard Web page names when they access a Web site. If the browser doesn't find one of the standard filenames, then it displays a listing of your site with all its files in a directory format. An example of this can be seen in Figure 125, or you can go to the **http://www.compuology.com/test/** Web site and see an example.

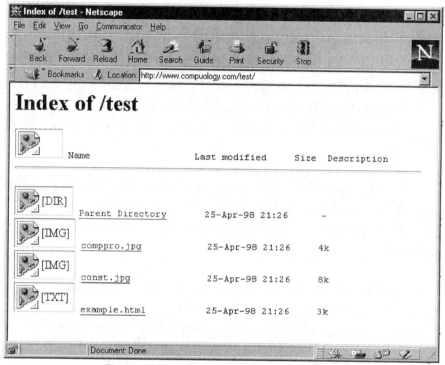

Figure 125: Web directory without an *index.html* file

Now comes the hardest part of creating your own Web site–deciding what information you want to include. Generally, your site will be made up of many separate pages all linked together. You can think of your Web site like a book with a table of contents, chapters, indexes, appendices, etc.

You must also decide on the layout that you want to use. Do not worry if you do not know how you want to set up your Web pages at first. You can always modify and add additional pages later. This is the beauty of the Internet. It is very easy to add or change data on your Web pages. You do not have to remember to include everything on your Web site when you first start out.

Even though you are starting this process with your home page, the steps you use in creating this Web page will generally be the same for each of the pages you create. The different types of Web pages will have various layouts and will be given different file names. Many of the pages you include could be pages you created from the programs in *Chapter 4*: "Converting Your Genealogical Data in Minutes," starting on page 63.

Some of the different types of Web pages that are typically seen on a personal genealogy Web site might be:

1. Home page (main page).

2. Surname pages (devoted to a particular surname).

3. Family history pages (Web pages with family stories).

4. Genealogy pages (data for family genealogies you have converted with one of the conversion programs).

5. Other Web sites (links to other genealogy sites).

6. Personal information (pages with personal interests of yourself and other family members).

As we discussed in *Chapter 2*: "Easing Into the Language of Web Pages," your Web pages need to be formatted using the HTML language. The first thing you need to put on your page is the title. Since we are going to start with your home Web page, you may want to give it a title as simple as "Richard's Genealogy Home Page."

Web pages are made up of two basic sections: the head and body. The head section contains a lot of information used by Web browsers and search engines and generally is not visible when you view the Web page. The body section contains the information you see when you view a Web page. An example of a very simple Web page, with its HTML codes, is shown on the next page (see Figure 126).

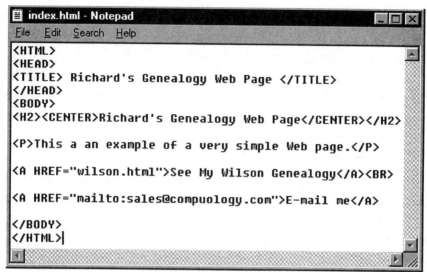

Figure 126: sample Web page

Here are the HTML codes for the sample Web page in Figure 126:

<HTML> This simply lets the Web browser software know that this is a HTML document; in other words, it is suitable for viewing or displaying on the World Wide Web portion of the Internet.

<HEAD> This code indicates that what follows is for the header section of the Web page (anything in this section won't show on the main Web page when it is displayed with a Web browser). Generally, the information included in the head section of a Web page is used by either the Web browser or a search engine.

<TITLE> The text that follows the <TITLE> code (in this case "Richard's Genealogy Web Page") won't show on the main Web page (because it is inside the <HEAD> section); however, the title "Richard's Genealogy Web Page" will show at the top of the Web browser's screen and will be the name given to the Web page when someone "bookmarks" the page or adds it to their "favorites." It will also be the name that most search engines will assign to the Web page when indexed.

\<BODY\>   This section contains the portion of the Web page that will be displayed by the Web browser when someone visits that Web page. It can include headings, text, links and graphic images. The formatted elements in the \<BODY\> section of your HTML document are the only portions that are visible with your Web browser.

\<CENTER\>   Text between these codes will be centered.

\<H2\>   Text between these codes is displayed in Header 2 size.

\<P\>   Text between these codes will be displayed as a separate paragraph (it automatically inserts a blank line before and after the text).

\<BR\>   Text after this code will be moved down one line.

\<A HREF="page.html">*Link***\</A\>**
        This is an example of a link that will send a person to another Web page. When the person clicks on the word between the > < signs (in this case "*Link*") the Web page referenced between the quote marks (in this case "*page.html*") will be opened in their Web browser.

\<A HREF="mailto:*me@myprovider.com*">*E-mail***\</A\>**
        This is an example of an e-mail link. When the person clicks on the name between the > < signs (in this case "*E-mail*") their e-mail program will start and the e-mail address after the mailto: reference above (in this case "*me@myprovider.com*") is inserted into the "To" field.

Figure 127 shows how this Web page will look when viewed with Microsoft's Internet Explorer.

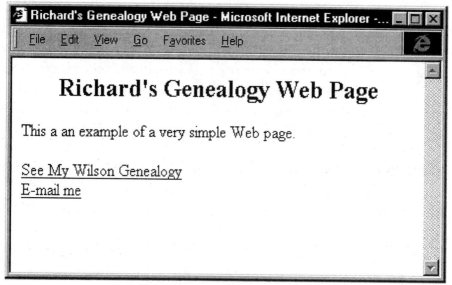

Figure 127: basic Web page example

 Learn by example: Most browsers allow you to view the source of the Web page you are viewing (the formatting the page's author wrote and which your browser uses to display the Web page). To view the source codes, you would select the "Source," "Page Source," or "View Source," menu item on either the "View" or "File" pull-down menu (depending on the specific browser you're running). This will display the HTML code for the page you are viewing. When you find a Web page with an item or feature you would like to use on your Web page (but do not know how to do it in HTML), view the source coding for that page so you can see exactly how it was done.

Setting Up Links and Directories

One of the most popular features on Web pages are hyperlinks that allow visitors to simply "click" on those links to navigate around your Web site. These links can be to another Web page on your own site or to a different Web site. Links can also be set up to show the visitor a photograph, play a sound, or open an e-mail message window.

One of the decisions you face is how your Web pages will be linked together. You also need to consider what external links you want to include on your pages. In this section, the various types of links that are available for you to use will be discussed. Examples will be given on how to set up these different types of links.

Richard
Says:

Many people have a tendency to put nothing on their site but links to other sites. Links to other sites are important, but you need to make sure your Web site also has good content. I have heard many people complain that all they can find are pages that take you to other pages that take you to other pages–and none of them contain any real data.

So, when creating your pages, do not just put a small amount of genealogical data on your Web pages. Also consider putting some of those family stories you have in your word processor. Or, how about putting images of those old family documents, perhaps old bible pages or marriage certificates, you have scanned. If you are a typical genealogist, you have a wealth of information you should share with others.

Internal Links

The first type of link to consider for your pages is an internal link. Such a link allows the visitor to jump from one place to another on the same Web page. This is especially helpful if you have a Web page that is several screens long. Without internal links, a person would have to scroll down the page to find the information they are interested in.

An example of a Web page with internal links would be a genealogy society page with an index of features at the top. An index of features shows the visitor what is available on that Web site (see Figure 128). The visitor simply has to "click" on the highlighted, underlined word in the index of features at the top of the page and they will be taken down to the place where the information is located.

Figure 128: Index (internal links to later portions of the Web page)

An internal link requires two codes to function. A "target" code (specifying where you want to jump to on that Web page) and a "reference" code (the link you want to jump from). The correct codes for the first internal link listed in the example in Figure 128 are:

The target code the reference will jump to is:
<A NAME="about"> About This Chapter</A>.

The link or reference code is:
<A HREF="#about">About This Chapter</A>.

Internal links are useful on most types of Web pages. They can be mixed with external links. The visitor cannot tell which links are internal and which are external when looking at the index of features for that Web page.

External Links

External links take the visitor to another Web page, file, graphic or program. This Web page, file, graphic, or program, may be stored on your provider's server (local) or they may be on another computer (remote). These links are used to let the visitor jump (or surf) from one page on the Internet to another. This is the type of link you will use to connect all of your Web pages together.

External links also allow graphics, sounds, and video clips to be linked to your Web pages. You use external links to link your Web page to other sites on the Internet that you feel are important.

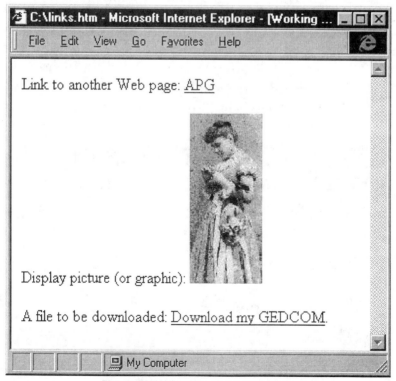

Figure 129: Web page using external links

There are many different types of external links. Figure 129 shows an example of three different types of external links. The correct codes for the different types of external links used in Figure 129 are:

Link to another Web page:

<A HREF="**http://www.apgen.org/~apg/**">APG</A>

> In this example the part within the quotes is the electronic address of the Web page your browser will take you to if you click on the word "APG," which shows as highlighted and underlined text on the Web page.

Display picture (or graphic):

<IMG SRC="ganny.jpg" ALT="Photo of Ganny - 57 K">

> In this example, *"ganny.jpg"* is the name of the graphic file that will be displayed as the Web page loads (as seen in Figure 123). "Photo of Ganny - 57 K" is the title of the image that will be displayed as the graphic loads, or if the visitor has the graphics feature of their Web browser off (see Figure 130).

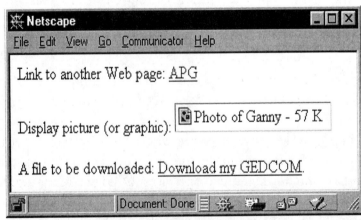

Figure 130: graphics turned off

A file to be downloaded:

<A HREF="myfile.ged">Download my GEDCOM</A>

> In this example, "*myfile.ged*" is the file that will be downloaded to the visitor's hard drive when they "click" on the "Download my GEDCOM" link that will be highlighted and underlined.

There are also two different methods of indicating where the files are located that the hyperlinks point to: relative and absolute. The differences between these two methods of links are in the paths to where the files are located. Here is an example of the two ways of referring to the file *wilson.htm*, located in my main Web directory **http://www.compuology.com/richard/**.

Relative link:

<A HREF="**wilson.htm**">Wilson Genealogy</A>

Absolute Link:

<A HREF="**http://www.compuology.com/richard/wilson.htm**"> Wilson Genealogy</A>

Both links will operate in the same way. The relative link has a few advantages. First, it is much easier to input only the file's name, instead of the full URL. Second, if you ever have to relocate your Web pages, you will not have to change all the links. Relative links look for the Web page only in the directory where the Web page is located. In the above relative link example, the link would only work if there was a file *wilson.htm* in the same directory as the page containing the link.

Any links to Web pages on other servers must always be entered as absolute links.

You can also use relative links to refer to files in other directories on your Web server. To point to a graphic file in a "graphic" sub-directory off of your main directory, you would use the following.

<IMG SRC="graphics/ganny.jpg" ALT="Photo of Ganny - 57 K">

You simply add the name of the subdirectory and the forward slash (/) before the graphic file name.

You can also refer to files in a lower directory on your Web server. Here is an example:

The Web page that contains the link is in:
   http://www.compuology.com/richard/wilson/

You want to point to graphic file in the directory:
   http://www.compuology.com/richard/

Use the following code:

<IMG SRC="../ganny.jpg" ALT="Photo of Ganny - 57 K">

The " . . / " before the name of the file tells the Web browser to look down one directory from the current directory the Web page is in for the file that is referenced.

Mail Links

Mail links (Mailto links) are another special type of external link. When a visitor clicks on a mail link, they start the "Mailto" program routine. This will open their mail program's dialog box and allow the visitor to send an e-mail message to the e-mail address contained in that mail link.

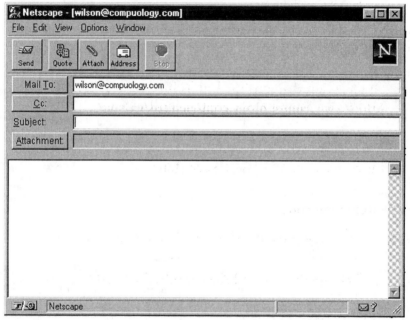

Figure 131: Netscape - Mailto dialog box

Figure 131 shows what the Netscape Mailto dialog box looks like. Once the box opens up, it will have the e-mail address that was contained in the link in the "Mail To:" field. All you have to do is add a subject line and your message, then click on the "Send" button.

Graphic Formats Supported on the Web

Now that you have decided what type of Web pages you are going to create, you will want to add some graphics to make your pages more interesting. You should consider putting some old family photos with your genealogical data to make your family tree come alive for visitors. Many of the conversion programs covered in this book allow you to add some types of graphics to the Web pages they create.

The first thing you need to know is that not all graphic formats can be used to display images on Web pages. There are two basic graphic formats used on the Web: JPG (pronounced Jay-Peg) and GIF (pronounced Jiff). A third format has recently been developed. It is called PNG but is not yet supported by many browsers. This chapter will cover each of these graphic formats in more detail.

Richard
Says:

When you consider putting graphics on your Web pages, they may be graphics you have already scanned or perhaps saved in a different graphics format. You will need to convert your graphic images to either GIF or JPG format so you can use them on your Web pages. There are many graphic conversion programs available to accomplish this. I personally use the LView Pro program <http://www.lview.com/> which converts graphic files to different formats, creates transparent GIFs, and performs screen captures.

Graphic Workshop <**http://www.mindworkshop.com/alchemy/gwspro.html**> is another image utility available that can view and convert between different image formats.

GIF Format

The Graphical Interchange Format (GIF) is much older than JPG. It was introduced by CompuServe Corporation in 1987. It has been used extensively on the Internet and is supported by almost all browsers that can handle graphics. It also allows transparency (for a definition of "Transparency," see page 161). Images stored in the GIF format have the extension of *.gif* (i.e., *baby.gif*). The GIF format allows a palette maximum of 256 colors, so it works best for line drawings, calligraphy, and cartoons.

A graphic saved in GIF format is usually larger in size than one saved in JPG format. As you can see from the two identical photos below (Figures 132 and 133), the GIF photo requires 676 KB of space, while the same graphic stored as a JPG takes only 84KB of storage space. The size difference is important because the amount of Web space you have will be limited. Though graphic pictures stored in GIF format will take up more space on your Web site, they may load faster because the computer doesn't have to un-compress the image.

Figure 132: *Baby.jpg* - 84 KB

Figure 133: *Baby.gif* - 676 KB

GIF does not work well for storing full-color or gray-scale scanned photographs. Anything with a continuous variation in color (such as highlighted or shaded areas) will be represented better and with less space in JPG format.

The GIF format is much better for images with only a few distinct colors (scanned documents such as wills, bible records, etc.). A GIF file for such images will usually be smaller than the same image in JPG format.

The GIF format does a much better job of displaying very sharp edges on drawings. Plain black-and-white images should always be stored in a GIF format. Half toned photo images are also suitable for saving as GIF files.

As mentioned before, Web pages with lots of graphics load very slowly. This can be very irritating to your visitors. There is one method of displaying photographs on your Web pages that will not slow down the viewing of your Web pages as much. That is to put small (thumbnail size) GIF images on your page that are linked to larger sized pictures of the same image. When the person viewing the Web page clicks on the thumbnail sized image, their browser will load and display the larger image.

Transparency

Transparent graphics are often used on the Internet. GIF format supports transparent images. One of the first things you will probably want to learn when putting together your Web site is how to create transparent backgrounds for GIF images. By making the background transparent, you will see only the image itself on the Web page. This is important when you are using a graphic background and you have a logo or simple graphic that you want to include. Without transparency, you will see a white square around the graphic (see Figure 134). With transparency, you see the background showing through the logo (see Figure 135).

There are many methods of converting an existing image you have to a transparent image. Here are links to a couple of tutorials on how to convert GIF images to transparent GIF images:

▲ A tutorial on creating transparent GIF images using the shareware LView Pro program, by Randy Ralph **<http://www.iconbazaar.com/tutorials/>**

▲ Here is another tutorial, by Jasc Software titled "How to create transparent GIF images using Paint Shop Pro, version 3.11 or newer." **<http://jasc.com/transtip.html>**

As you can see by comparing the examples on the next page, there are times when a transparent image will look much nicer on your Web page (especially if you are the genealogist responsible for setting up the WAGS Web page). Transparent images allow your Web page elements (both text and graphics) to flow and work together better.

Figure 134: Non-transparent GIF

Figure 135: Transparent GIF

JPG Format

The Joint Photographic Experts Group (also known as JPEG) is a compressed graphic file format which is excellent for most real images (full-color or gray-scale images or photos). The JPG format is superior for storing any image with a continuous variation in color (such as highlighted or shaded areas). This format can also reduce the size of stored images by a factor of ten or more. There is, however, a small amount of degradation in the image when it is uncompressed later for viewing. Images stored in the JPG format have the extension of *.jpg* or *.jpeg* (i.e., *image.jpg* or *image.jpeg*).

You need to be aware that the JPG format does not do a good job of displaying very sharp edges on drawings. Sharp edges tend to come out blurred. Sharp edges are rare in scanned photographs, but are common in drawings with borders or overlaid text (such as scanned marriage and birth certificates).

There are two reasons to use the JPG format rather than GIF format for storing (saving) your images. First, JPG makes the files smaller so they take less space on your Web site. Secondly, JPG can store an image in 16 million colors, while GIFs can only store 256 or fewer colors. One drawback to using JPG files is that JPG does not support transparency.

Unless a very fast computer is used to view the graphic file, large JPG images are noticeably slower loading on the Internet. This is because the receiving computer must uncompress the graphic file as the page is loaded (displayed) on your computer.

PNG Format

Portable Network Graphics (PNG) is a new graphic format which improves on the GIF format. It permits truecolor images, indexed-color images, grayscale images, and supports transparency. It also does a good job of compressing images for storage or electronic transfer. Images stored in the PNG format have the extension of *.png* (i.e., *image.png*).

Although the PNG image format was approved on October 14, 1996, it is not yet supported by many Web browsers (see Figure 136).

Browsers that currently support PNG are:

Microsoft's Internet Explorer - version 4.0b1 and later. Limited support; read-only; no progressive display; no alpha support; no simple transparency (uses gray background color even though default page color is white); no gamma support.

Netscape Navigator [Netscape Communications] - version 2.0 and later with plug-ins; native PNG support is expected in version 5.0. Note that Netscape plug-ins currently do not support true inlined images; they only support images with Netscape's EMBED tag--which is not usable by most other browsers.

SPRYNET Mosaic [SPRY/CompuServe] - all versions; read-only; full gamma support.

WinCIM /CompuServe software - version 2.0.1 and later; read-only; progressive display of interlaced images (replicating method).

Figure 136: Browsers supporting PNG graphics

Sounds and Video for Your Web Site

There are two basic methods of adding sounds or video clips to your Web site. One method is to add sound or video that automatically plays in the background when someone visits (views) one of your Web pages. The second method is to use sound or video files that a person can click on to hear, view, or download. Sound and video files are generally very large and take up a lot of space on your Web site. You will want to use them sparingly. They may also take a long time to download to your visitor's computer.

There are several different programs that allow you to put automatic sound or video on your site (See the list in Figure 137). You should know that in order to be able to use these files, the visitor must have the corresponding program (or Web browser plug-in) installed on their computer.

Some sound programs can be found on the Web at:

AUDIOACTIVE:
http://www.audioactive.com/

Crescendo:
http://www.liveupdate.com/crescendo.html

Macromedia Shockwave:
http://www.macromedia.com/shockwave/

RealAudio's RealPlayer:
http://www.realaudio.com/products/player/get.html

SSEYO® Koan® Pro 2:
http://www.sseyo.com/kprobroc.html

Figure 137: Sound/video programs available for the Internet

If you want music playing in the background, streaming is important. Streaming allows music to be heard while the page is being downloaded (viewed). Without streaming, Web site visitors must wait for the entire file to be transferred to their computer. Following is a brief description of the programs listed in Figure 137.

✧   AUDIOACTIVE is based on very interesting technology. It uses MPEG audio coding to squeeze the audio file down to less than 10% of its original size. This is a good choice if you have size limitations for storing your Web pages on your server.

✧   Crescendo is a Web music player. It is available as an add-on for the Netscape and Microsoft Web browsers. It lets a visitor listen to MIDI music as they browse your Web site.

✧   Shockwave by Macromedia delivers high quality interactive multimedia, graphics, and streaming audio (from hi-fi to CD quality) on your Web site. It gives you fully interactive multimedia including dynamic animations, graphics, text, and audio.

✧   RealAudio's RealPlayer lets you play live and on-demand RealAudio and RealVideo without download delays. It provides streaming audio and video.

✧   SSEYO's Koan Pro gives you the ability to create background music. Koan sound bytes can play up to eight hours yet average only 7 Kb per file. This makes it a good choice for Web pages/sites with space limitations.

The other way to add sound files to your site is to add external links (hyperlinks) to the sound or video clips on your Web site. Then visitors can click on the link to hear the sounds.

The correct formats for adding a sound or video clips to your Web pages are:

<A HREF="sound.wav">Download sound clip</A>

> The sound file named "*sound.wav*" is the one that will be downloaded to the visitor's hard drive, or opened in their sound program, when they click on the link called "Download sound clip."

<A HREF="video.mov">Download video clip</A>

> The video file named "*video.mov*" is the one that will be downloaded to the visitor's hard drive, or opened in their video program, when they click on the link called "Download video clip."

Web "Hit" Counters

A "Hit" counter is a code that is included on your Web page. It keeps track of how many times your page is downloaded (viewed) by Web browsers, thus indicating how popular the site is. I'm sure you have seen many of them on the Web pages you have visited. They usually say something like "You are visitor number 1,000 to my Web site since January 4, 1999." A Web counter can give you a very good indication of when your site isn't getting enough advertising.

Hit counters are server specific. If you copy the code for a hit counter from another Web site to your Web page, it probably won't work. A web counter is actually a small program which must be installed on and run from a server connected to the Internet. The best way to add a hit counter is to use one offered by your Web space provider's server. Your provider will let you know if they offer hit counters and give you the correct coding so the counter will operate properly.

If your Web space provider doesn't offer a hit counter, you will have to use a separate hit counter service. Some hit counter services require you to include their ads on your Web pages in exchange for using their service. Figure 138 lists a few hit counter services available.

A few hit counter Web sites are:

PR-Tracker's FREE Webpage Hit Counter:
    http://www.prtracker.com/freecounter.html

JCount Free Counter Creation Page:
    http://www.jcount.com/

Pagecount :
    http://www.pagecount.com/

PIN's Guide to free Web counters:
    http://www.servanet.net/pinsguide/count/index.htm

WebSideStory:
    http://www.hitbox.com/

Figure 138: Hit counters available on the Internet

Meta Tags

Meta tags are a special type of HTML tag. They are used to provide certain types of information about the Web page to the local server or the Web browser. These tags are not visible on the Web page nor do they affect how the page is displayed. They are normally used to provide such information as who created the page, what the Web page is about, and which keywords best represent the page's content. Most search engines use this information when building their indexes.

Meta tags should always be placed in the head section of the HTML document between the actual <HEAD></HEAD> tags and before the <BODY> tag. Figure 139 shows the typical use of the Meta tag using the NAME element.

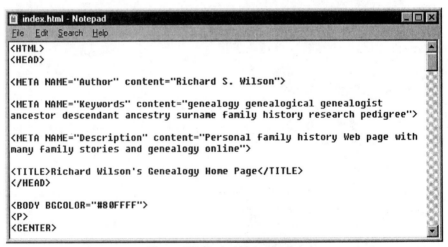

Figure 139: Typical Meta tag use

The two META NAME attributes that are most important to your Web page are the "keyword" and "description" attributes. These are used by the search engines to index your page using the keywords you specifically tell it, along with a description of the site that you yourself get to write.

The correct format for the keywords attribute is:
<META NAME ="keywords" CONTENT="genealogy, family history, research, ancestry, WILSON, FELDER, genealogist">

By the way, do not think you can make your Web site come up first on the search engines by using the same word repeated over and over. Most search engines have refined their spiders to ignore multiple uses of a word.

The correct format for the description attribute is:
<META NAME="description" CONTENT="This page is about my family history. I have been researching the Wilson and Felder family lines for many years.">

Make sure you also use several of your keywords in the description of your Web site. While you are at it, you may want to include the same description enclosed in comment tags just for the search engines that do not look at the META tags.

An HTML comment tag is formatted like this:
<!--// This page is about my family history. I have been researching the Wilson and Felder family lines for years. //--!>

This section is just a brief description of a few of the uses for META tags. If you want to learn even more about Meta tags, check out one of these online tutorials:

Galactus' META info page:
     http://www.stack.nl/~galactus/html/meta.html

Vancouver's META Tag Page:
     http://vancouver-webpages.com/META/

WebDeveloper.com META Tag Resource Page:
  http://www.webdeveloper.com/categories/html/html_metatag_res.html

If you'd like some assistance with creating your Meta tags, check out Andrew Daviel's form-based tag generator. You simply fill in the blanks on his form and he will generate the correct Meta tags for you.
  http://vancouver-webpages.com/VWbot/mk-metas.html

Guest Books

Guest books are a great way for people to leave you messages about your Web site without having to send you an e-mail message. They can just "fill-in the blanks" in your guest book (see samples of entries in Figure 141). There are two ways to set up a guest book on your Web site.

One method is to locate a guest book written in CGI script and install it on your Web provider's server computer. To do this, you must have access to their CGI directory. For more information about using CGI scripts, see "CGI Scripts" in *Appendix C*, on page 267.

The second method would be to set up a guest book on your Web site from a guest book service provider. A couple of examples of providers are listed in Figure 140.

A few guest book service providers are:

Guestbook*Star:
> http://www.webgenie.com/Software/Guestar/

Guestbook*Star is a shareware guestbook created by Web Genie. It allows you to create a guestbook instantly without any programming or CGI knowledge. Registration cost for this program is $29.00 (US).

GuestWorld:
> http://saturn.guestworld.tripod.lycos.com/

You can get a free guest book at GuestWorld. They provide guest books for over 1.1 million Web site owners around the world.

Figure 140: Guest book providers on the Internet

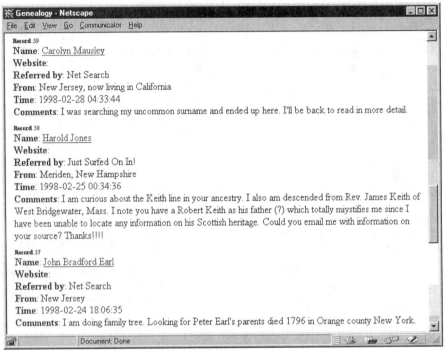

Figure 141: Sample guest book entries

Richard Says:

I have made some great contacts through my guest book. Many times people will fill out a guest book entry rather than take the time to locate my e-mail address and send me an e-mail. You should definitely consider having a guest book on your Web pages.

Proofread, Inspect and Validate Your Pages

After creating your Web pages, you need to check each page carefully to make sure there are no problems with them. Check for spelling errors, layout, and HTML coding problems. It is easier to check these problems before you upload your pages onto the Internet.

If you have a word processor, simply load the Web page into it and run the spell checker. If you save the page after spell checking, select DOS or ASCII text as the type of file you wish to save.

Layout and HTML coding errors can be checked by loading the page into your Web browser from your hard drive. Start your Web browser and do the following:

Internet Explorer:
> Select "Open" from the "File" pull-down menu, then select "Browse" to locate the file on your hard disk. Your Web page will then be displayed on your Web browser screen.

Netscape Communicator:
> Select "Open Page" from the "File" pull-down menu, then select "Choose File" to locate the file on your hard disk. Your Web page will then be displayed on your Web browser screen.

If there are HTML coding errors, they will be very evident. You may notice that the page is not laid out properly, or the text does not look correct, or some of the graphics didn't load.

Transferring
Your Pages
Onto the Internet

Chapter 6

Locating Web Space

Now that you have decided what information you want and have created and checked your Web pages, you need to store these files on a Web server (a computer connected to the Internet 24-hours a day) so that they can be accessed by others.

Can't I use my own computer to store my Web pages?

Not usually. Your computer would have to be connected to the Internet 24-hours a day and you would have to run special software (such as Unix or Windows NT) to allow your computer to act as a server. Most ISPs, although they offer you unlimited access, will not allow you to be connected 24-hours a day. In fact, most ISPs will disconnect your computer if you haven't made any active Internet access for 20-30 minutes. In addition, will your phone company allow you to tie up your telephone connection 24-hours a day? Some cable companies are allowing you to have Web pages accessible on your own computer. But remember, your computer would have to be on and connected 24-hours a day for this to work.

Depending on which server you decide to use, you may be limited with what you are able to include on your pages. All Web space providers are definitely not created equal.

Please be aware that there are hundreds of Web space providers on the Internet. There is no way this chapter can cover all of the features of these various providers.

When it comes to locating Web space for your genealogy Web site, you generally have three basic options available to you. Each of these have advantages and disadvantages. These are:

- *Your ISP's server*
- *One of the many free Web space sites*
- *A paid Web space provider*

Your ISP's Server

Many ISPs offer limited free Web space (usually 2-10 Megabytes) for their subscribing users. Check with your current ISP to see if they offer this service (usually they do not mention it unless you ask). You are already paying your ISP a monthly fee for dial-up access, you may as well take advantage of all the services they offer.

Advantages:

- Free Web space is usually included with your dial-up fee.
- Your pages usually will not contain advertizing.
- Usually you do not have a new user name and password to remember.

Disadvantages:

- Space is usually limited–additional space on their server may be very expensive.
- Their services may not have all of the features you want or need.
- Usually you cannot have your own domain name on your free site (www.yourname.com).

Even though your ISP offers you <u>free</u> space on their server, you may still decide to put your Web pages on a different server if you need more space than they allow. For example, when I first set up my Web site on Earthlink (my ISP), they gave me 2 Megabytes of free Web space (they now offer 6 Megabytes). However, I needed about 20 megabytes of Web space. I found I could get 20 megabytes on another server for a lot less than Earthlink wanted to charge me for the additional 18 megabytes of space (in fact I found a provider who gave me 40 megabytes of space for less money).

Free Web Space Sites

The second option is to get a free Web site with one of the many free Web space providers. Figure 142 contains a partial list of free providers.

Here are a few providers with free Web space:

Angelfire:
> http://www.angelfire.com/

Free Sites Network:
> http://www.fsn.net/index2.html

Geocities:
> http://www.geocities.com/join/freehp.html

Fortune City:
> http://www2.fortunecity.com/downtown/index.cgi

Tripod:
> http://homepager.tripod.com/

Figure 142: Free Web space providers on the Internet

Advantages:

- Web space is free (this is a great feature).
- Many use their own Web editors (this can make it easy for you to create your Web pages).
- Many use their own file transfer programs (this can make it easy for you to upload your Web pages to their site).

Disadvantages:

- Most require advertizing on your Web pages.
- They may not have all of the features you want or need.
- Usually you cannot use your own domain name.
- May require you to use only their Web editor (this can limit what you are able to put on your Web pages).
- They may require you to upload only files they create (this also limits what you can put on your Web pages).
- Web space is usually limited.

 Giant-List-O-Webspace:
http://www.ptialaska.net/~buechler/Brians/homepages.html

Although this page hasn't been updated since May 1997, it is still a good place to locate free Web space providers. It lists many providers and includes information such as the Server name, space limit, FTP access, upload ability, images allowed, PO mail address, CGI access, provided CGI scripts, server stability, and an overall rating for every site.

This is a great site where you can compare the features of many **free** Web space providers.

Free Web space sounds great, why would I ever want to pay for Web space?

Most free Web space providers require you to give them advertising space in return for Web space. Some people may not want to visit your Web site because of all the advertising. Also, some Web browsers may crash because of the java script that creates the advertising. In addition, sometimes people don't close the advertising properly, which can cause an overload of their computer's available memory.

Paid Web Space Providers

The third option is to rent Web space. Many Internet Web servers offer space for a monthly or annual fee. The cost depends somewhat on how much space you will need. Check the fees of several different providers. You will find these charges vary widely.

Advantages:

- You can use your own domain name (**www.yourname.com**).
- They require no advertizing on your Web pages.
- Space is unlimited (you can get as much as you can afford).
- They usually give you access to many additional features (CGI scripts, guest books, counters, and more).

Disadvantages:

- Web space on their server costs money.
- You may have to learn additional software (or programming) to take advantage of the extra features they offer.

Before you make your final decision on where to place your Web site, it would be a good idea for you to determine how much space you need. There is no reason to set up a Web site on a server that limits your space only to have to change servers because you do not have enough room for all of your files.

One way to check the total amount of Web space you need is to place all of the files you created into one directory or folder on your hard drive (make sure you include all the graphics and sound files). Check the total size of all the files in that directory or folder. Of course, you probably want more space than you actually need to allow for some growth (remember how fast your hard drive filled up?).

Once you have decided where you are going to be placing your Web site, you will need to transfer all of your files (Web pages, graphics, sound files, etc.) to their Internet server (computer). Normally, you will use a File Transfer Protocol (FTP) program to accomplish this. Be aware that some Web space providers require you to use only their software to upload your files to their Web site.

Working with Free Web Space Providers

Web space providers who offer free Web space are one of the most popular types of providers. However, you need to know that they usually operate a little differently than paid Web space providers. Usually they offer a simple type of Web page creation editor as part of their free service. In addition, you generally transfer your files to them with their own FTP software program.

Since building and transferring files to a free Web space provider is a little different, this section will demonstrate how easy it is to create and transfer Web pages to a free provider. It will guide you through getting and setting up your own Web space on Tripod (**http://www.tripod.com**). They offer you 11 megabytes of Web space for free.

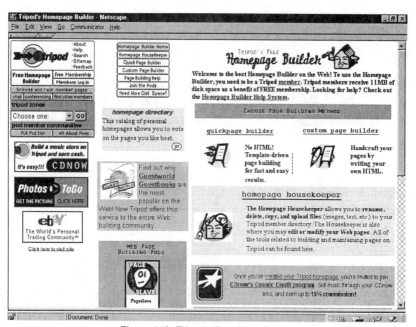

Figure 143: Tripod - Free Web Space

The first step is to access their Web site and request your Web space (see Figure 143). To get your free Web space, simply select the "member" link. You will then see the "Tripod Membership Sign-Up" screen (see Figure 144). You fill out the membership application and select the "Join" button.

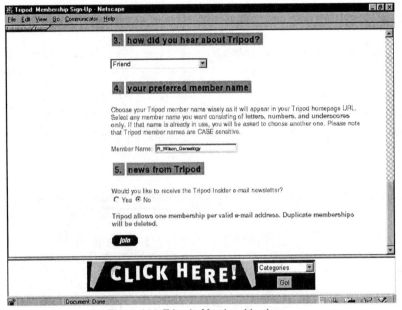

Figure 144: Tripod - Membership sign-up

Next you will be asked to select the "pod" where you want to create your Web site. A pod is simply the area of interest your site would best fit in, such as "Genealogy." You can create more than one Web site if you wish. To select an area, click on the box to the left of the area and a check mark will appear (See Figure 145). Once you have selected the area of interest, you select the "Submit" button. The screen in Figure 146 will appear.

Figure 145: Tripod - select area of interest

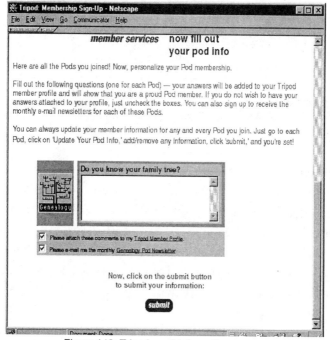

Figure 146: Tripod - pod information screen

From the screen in Figure 146, you can input a description or introductory comments about your new Web page. Next, you click on the "Select" button. You will then see the welcome screen (see Figure 147). From this screen, select the "Free Homepage Builder" hyperlink.

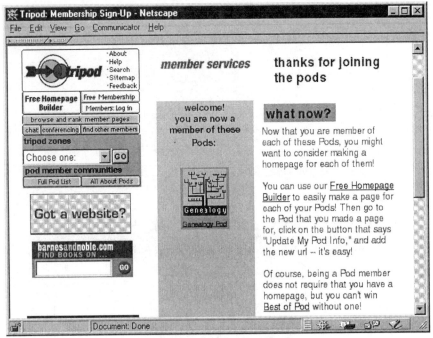

Figure 147: Tripod - What Now?

This will take you back to the screen shown in Figure 143. You can select from either the "Quick Page Builder" or the Custom Page Builder" links. If you select the quick page builder link, you will see the Quick Page Builder screen (see Figure 148). The first step is to name your Web page. If it is the main Web page for your site, give it the name "*index.html*" and click on the "Use This Filename" button. The "Choose a Layout" screen will appear (see Figure 149). Choose the style of layout you want to use by clicking on the "Select This Layout" button under the example.

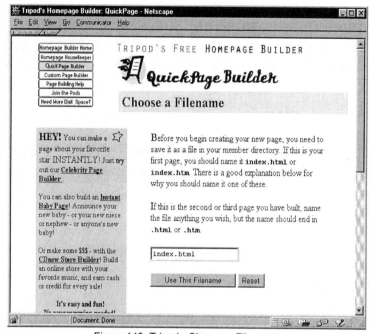

Figure 148: Tripod - Choose a Filename

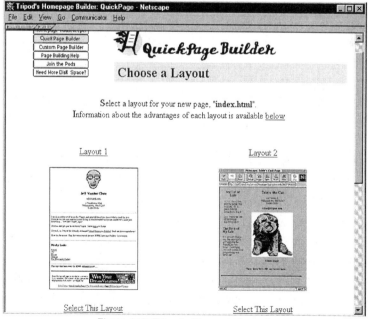

Figure 149: Tripod - Choose a Layout

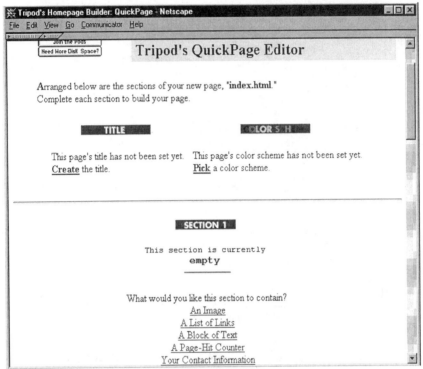

Figure 150: Tripod - QuickPage Editor

From the QuickPage Editor (see Figure 150), you can create the sections of the Web page design you selected, one at a time, by selecting the hyperlink for each of the various sections. You do not have to put something in every section. As you can see in Figure 150, there are many different items you can put in each section of the Web page you are creating. As you select each section, you will also see the HTML codes that are required to make the Web page (see Figure 151).

As you create each section, you click on the "OK" button. Once you have created all the sections you want, you need to click on the "Save Page" button. The "Page Saved!" screen will appear (see Figure 152).

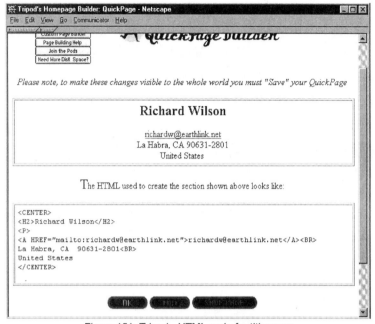

Figure 151: Tripod - HTML code for title page

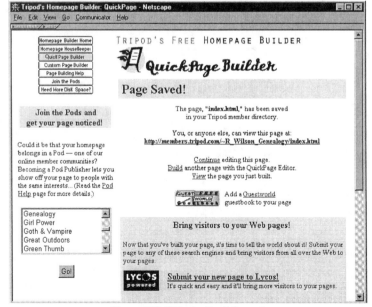

Figure 152: Tripod - Page Saved!

From the "Page Saved!" screen, you will be given the URL for your newly created Web page. You can see your new Web page by clicking on the hyperlink with the URL for your page or the "View" hyperlink. Once you click on either of these, you will see the Web page you have created (see Figure 153).

Figure 153: Tripod - home page

Once you have signed up for a Web page with Tripod, you will be sent an e-mail message with your user name and password (see Figure 154). Make sure you save these. It is a good idea to print out a paper copy of this message, as well as save the e-mail. This user name and password will be required to make corrections or additions to your Web pages later.

Tripod also offers a premium membership for a fee. This membership gives you many additional features (see Figure 155).

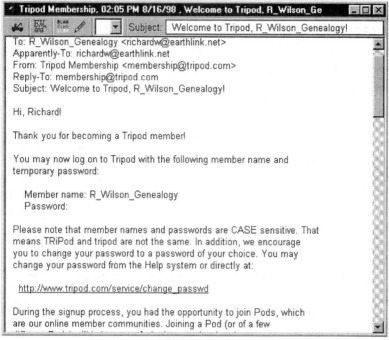

Figure 154: Tripod - e-mail message

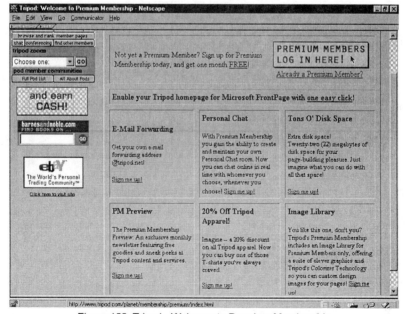

Figure 155: Tripod - Welcome to Premium Membership

From the "Home Page Housekeeper" screen (see Figure 156) you can create additional Web pages. You can also perform standard FTP functions, such as upload files or create subdirectories. You can also move, erase, or rename files.

To create a sub-directory on your new Web site, select the "Create a new subdirectory" from the pull-down menu and click on the "go!" button. The "Create a new Subdirectory" screen will appear (see Figure 157). You then type in the name of the subdirectory you want to create and click on the "Use This Filename" button and the directory will be created.

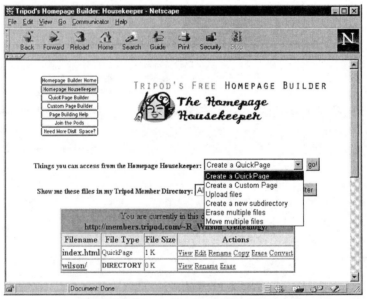

Figure 156: Tripod - Homepage Housekeeper

If you want to write your own HTML pages, you can also use the "Page Editor" (see Figure 158). This is available by selecting "Create a Custom Page" from the pull-down menu, and clicking on the "go!" button (see figure 156).

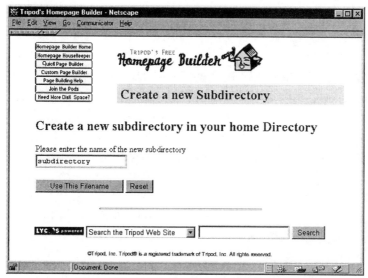

Figure 157: Tripod - Create a new Subdirectory

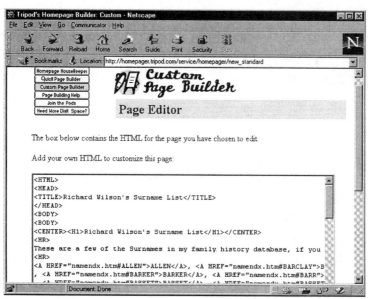

Figure 158: Tripod - Page Editor

Working with Your Web Space Provider

If you chose your own ISP or a paid provider, you need to know how to transfer your files to them. When you first set up your account, they will send you instructions for accessing their server, usually in an e-mail message. Make sure you print out a copy of the message and also archive it (save it) so you can refer back to it later, if you need to.

To upload your files to your Web space provider, you will need a user name, a password, and the location of the FTP directory they have set up for you to use. If you are using space on your Internet service provider (ISP), you need to be aware that the user name and password they give you for accessing the FTP site may not be the same user name and password you use for your Internet connection with them.

Your provider will assign a directory for you to use and let you know what your URL will be for your site. Typically, the address they give you will have a tilde [~] in front of your user name. A tilde is on the key to the left of the numeral 1 key on your keyboard (you must press the `Shift` key to type it). For example, the Earthlink login name assigned to me was richardw, so the address to my Earthlink home page is: **http://home.earthlink.net/~richardw/**.

Once you have connected to the remote computer (server) of your Web space provider, you will upload your files into the directory that was assigned to you by them (do not worry, we will cover **how** to connect and transfer files later on in this chapter–see page 200). You can also create subdirectories under your main directory to help organize your files, just like you do on your computer's hard disk.

When I received my free Web space with my Earthlink account, I was assigned the **ftp://ftp-www.earthlink.net/webdocs/** directory for my files. This means I place my Web home page (*index.html*) file into that location (upload it to that site). However, if you want to view my

Web page, you would not use the FTP address, but the address of **http://home.earthlink.net/~richardw/** into your Web browser.

Why you would want to use **http://home.earthlink.net/~richardw/** if you could have the URL of **http://www.wilson.com/**? An address such as this is called a "domain name." To have this type of address, you must register it. There are a few restrictions and requirements for getting a domain name.

1. Make sure no one else has registered that name—it must be unique. You can search the domain name database at **http://www.networksolutions.com/cgi-bin/whois/whois/**.

2. Register your domain name with InterNIC (this costs money)

3. Make sure your Internet space provider will allow you use the domain name you have registered.

InterNIC registration services is located at: **http://www.networksolutions.com/**

To check to see if a domain name is available, use the Whois server at **http://www.networksolutions.com/cgi-bin/whois/whois/**

When you register your own domain name, your Web site becomes a "Virtual Server" (**www.yourdomain.com**). When you have your Web site under someone else's domain name, your Web site is considered a "Non-virtual Server" (**www.yourprovider.com/~yoursite**).

If you have your own domain name, you will not have to change the URL of your home page ever again. Normally, your Web page address is dependant on your Web space provider. If you decide to change to another Web server, your URL will change.

Richard Says:

Sometimes you do not even have to change Web space providers for them to change your URL. When I first set up my Web pages on Earthlink's server, the URL I was assigned was **http://www.earthlink.net/~richardw**. After about six months, they informed me they would be changing the address of my URL to **http://home.earthlink.net/~richardw/**. They had decided to move all the free Web pages to another directory on their server.

Another major advantage to having your own domain name is that your e-mail address can be setup to use your domain name. Consequently, your e-mail address will always stay the same, even if you move your Web pages to another server. If you select **http://www.myroots.com** as your domain name, you can use *<yourname@myroots.com>* as your e-mail address.

What does it cost to have your own domain name? Currently, it is $35.00 per year paid directly to InterNIC. You must pay the first two years ($70.00) when you register the domain name the first time. Some Web space providers also charge a fee for setting up your domain own name.

You can register your own domain name even if you do not yet have a Web space provider. There are a limited number of domain names available. If you find a domain name that you really want and the name is still available, you may want to go ahead and register it. When you are ready to create your Web site, the name will still be available for you.

Once you set up your Web site, you will want to set up sub-directories under your main Web directory. You do not want to store all of your files in one main directory. You can set up a different sub-directory for each of the surnames you will be putting on your Web site. You could have a "Wilson" directory with all your Wilson Web pages and a "Smith" directory with all of your Smith Web pages, etc. You can also create a separate directory to keep all of your graphics. Also, some of the Web page creation programs require their Web pages to be put in separate directories. Figure 159 shows an example of a typical Web directory structure, with "richard" as the main Web directory.

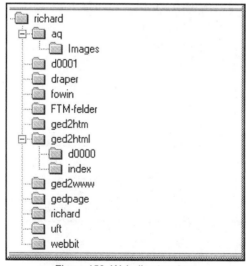

Figure 159: Web directory tree

File Transfer Protocol (FTP)

File Transfer Protocol is a program for transferring files between computers on the Internet. It is also the set of rules that govern how files are copied from one computer to another.

FTP makes it possible for you to transfer your own files onto a remote computer (server) once you have been given the proper user name and password to access that server. You can use any Web browser to download files from the Internet; however, you must use a program capable of uploading (with the use of FTP) to transfer your Web pages (HTML files) onto the Internet.

You can download a freeware or shareware FTP program from the Internet. You can purchase a commercial version of an FTP program. Or, you can use one of the integrated programs (such as Netscape Communicator Web browser or Hot Dog Pro HTML editor). Once you have installed this software, you are ready to transfer files.

 Not all FTP programs are created equal. It is a good idea to try one or two shareware FTP programs and see how you like their features before you spend money to purchase one.

If you are a Macintosh user, you can download a software program called Fetch. Fetch 2.1.2 is an easy-to-use Macintosh shareware program for FTP (see page 212). Windows users can download a program called WS_FTP, available in Windows or Windows 95/98 versions (see page 203).

No matter which program you chose to transfer your files to your Web server, they need to be transferred with the proper method. Your Web pages (the *.htm* or *.html* files) need to be transferred as "ASCII" or "text" files. The image and multimedia files for your Web pages need to be uploaded as "Binary" or "Raw Data" files.

Your files must all use standard extensions (GIF files must end with the suffix ".gif", JPG files should end in ".*jpg*" or ".*jpeg*", HTML files should end with ".*html*" or ".*htm*", etc.). This way the correct "Content Type" will be sent to the Web browser when the data is requested. Otherwise, the Web browser will not know how to handle the files.

 You may find it difficult to logon to some FTP sites, particularly during the hours the Internet is the busiest. You need to be aware that most FTP sites set a limit on the number of people who can logon to their server at one time. So, if you find you have trouble connecting, try again at a later time.

Your Web pages, images, and other files will reside in the subdirectory that was assigned to you when your account was set up. All documents that are to be accessible via your Web pages must reside under this directory hierarchy. You are free to organize your files in your own way under this directory. You are free to use whatever structure works best for you. If you created subdirectories under your main directory, you can place an *index.html* file in each of those directories. The reason you would want to do this is so you can use a URL such as **http://www.yourprovider.com/~yourloginname/otherdir/** to access that Web page.

When someone inputs the URL for your home page, their Web browser will automatically look in your main directory for the file *index.html*, *index.htm*, or *default.htm* and load it as your home page. The server will also look in that directory for any other HTML files you specify.

Remember, depending on the type of server, your home page address will be:

(Virtual Server)
   http://www.yourdomain.com/

(Non-Virtual Server)
   http://www.netgate.net/~yourloginname/

For more information about FTP see:

Tutorials on FTP at EFF's *Guide to the Internet:*
   ftp://ftp.eff.org/pub/EFF/netguide.eff

Another source is the *FTP Tutorial:*
   http://EditorsDeskTop.com/ftpinfo1.html

Uploading With WS_FTP

WS_FTP LE is a very popular, easy to use, shareware FTP program. It is available to download from:

http://www.ipswitch.com/cgi/download_eval.pl?

Richard Says:

WS_FTP LE is my favorite FTP program It is available for both Windows and Windows 95/98.

Any time you want to upload files to the Internet with WS_FTP, you must first connect to your Internet service provider. This program can only connect to an FTP site after you logon to your provider.

- Next, start the program by clicking on its icon. The main program screen will open with the "Session Properties" screen over it (see Figure 160). If this is the first time you are using the program, you will see data there from another setup. You will need to set up a new session profile.

- Click on the "New" button to clear the fields

- Now you need to enter the following information:

Profile Na<u>me</u>:   Give it a name (such as My Web Server).

Host <u>N</u>ame/Address: Input the location of the FTP site your provider gave you to use (such as **ftp.yourprovider.com**).

Host T̲ype: Leave "Automatic detect."

U̲ser ID: Put in the user ID your Web server gave you.

P̲assword: Put in your password. (Note: for security
                            reasons, when you enter your password, each
                            character will appear on the screen as an *)

- Next to the password, check the box labeled "Sa̲ve Pwd." This
  will save your password so you do not have to type it in every
  time you want to use the program to logon to this site. (see
  Figure 161)

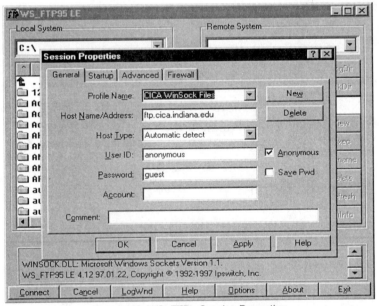

Figure 160: WS_FTP - Session Properties

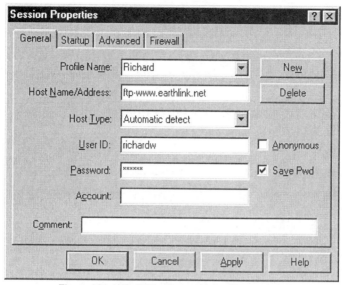

Figure 161: WS_FTP - General tab with user info

Figure 162: WS_FTP - Startup tab

• Select the "Startup" tab at the top of the box (see Figure 162). When you first set up a profile, the "Initial Remote Host Directory:" and "Initial Local Directory:" fields will be blank. You can leave them blank, as they are not necessary for the program to operate. Filling in these fields, however, will save you from having to change directories each time you logon to the site.

- In the "Initial Remote" field, enter the name of the directory where your Web pages will be stored on your provider's computer.

- In the "Initial Local" field, put the path to the location of your HTML files.

You will not need to use the "Advanced" tab. The "Firewall" tab also will not be needed, unless your FTP server requires you to upload through a firewall.

Once you have entered this data, click on the "OK" button to logon to the remote FTP server. The Session Properties screen will disappear. Your settings will be saved so you do not have to enter them again. The next time you start WS_FTP, just click the "OK" button to be connected to this site.

If you are connected to the site, you will get a message at the bottom of the screen that says "226 Transfer complete" (see Figure 163).

If you get a message which reads "Login failure," you have failed to connect. Try a second time. If you get another error message, make sure you have connected with your dialer program first and are still connected to the Internet. If the problem persists, try to connect at another time. If you are still unable to connect, contact your Web space provider with a description of the error message you are receiving.

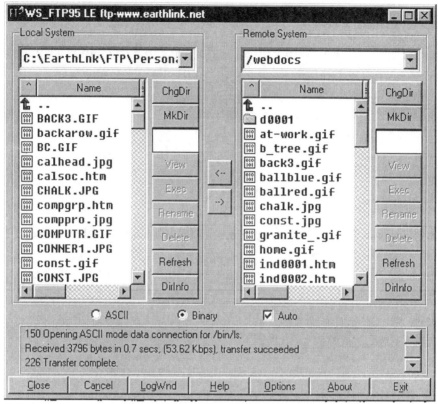

Figure 163: WS_FTP - main screen

Notice that the main program screen in Figure 163 has two windows side-by-side. The field at the top of each section indicates your current directory. The large boxes display the files and subdirectories (with a picture of a folder next to each file) that are found in the current directory. The ".." indicates there is a link to the directory just above the current directory. The left window shows your computer's hard drive directory. The right displays the FTP site's directory (the site on the Internet where you will be uploading your Web page files).

The function of the eight buttons on the side of each large box are:

ChgDir: To change directories (you can also change a directory by double-clicking on the directory name).

MkDir: To make a new directory.

View: Allows you to see a highlighted file using NotePad.

Exec: Run the file, if it is a program.

Rename: Allows you to rename the highlighted file or directory.

Delete: Allows you to delete the highlighted file or directory.

Refresh: Updates the list of files if changes have been made to a directory (e.g., if a new file was added or deleted).

DirInfo: Lists all of the file details in a NotePad window.

To transfer files:

- In the Local system section (left side) of the screen, change to the directory where the files you want to upload are stored.

- On the Remote system side, change to the directory location (or create the directories, if needed) where you want to place your Web pages.

- Highlight the files you wish to upload or download. (You can select multiple files by holding down the control <Ctrl> key when you select them.

- Once you have highlighted all the files you want to transfer, click the appropriate arrow to move them. To transfer files from your computer to the Internet, use the -> arrow (pointing toward the Remote system window). To transfer files from the Internet to your computer, click on the <− arrow (pointing toward the Local system window).

If you are going to be transferring both HTML files and graphic files, you must do two transfers because you need to select the proper format for the type of files you are going to upload. To transfer your text files (.htm, .html, or .ged files) select the ASCII radio button. To transfer image and audio files (.gif, .jpg, .wav, etc.), select the "Binary" radio button.

Once the transfer has been completed, you will see the files you have moved in the Remote system window (on the right side). When you have finished transferring your files with WS_FTP, be sure to press the "Close" or "Exit" button. Do not simply hang up or shut off your computer. As soon as your Web pages and graphics have been uploaded to the server, they can be viewed by anyone who connects to your Web site.

Remember, your main Web page should be saved as *index.html*. If you are using Windows 3.x you cannot give the file an *.html* suffix, so you need to upload the file as *index.htm* and then use the "Rename" button to change the page's name to *index.html*.

If you want to update an existing file, simply upload your new version of the file. You do not need to delete the old one first because the old file will be overwritten by the new version. You need to be aware that there is no warning before a file is overwritten, so be sure you are uploading the correct files into the correct location.

These are the basic steps for transferring files with the WS_FTP program. You can continue to upload files to your site in this manner as you create or make changes to your Web pages.

Uploading Files With Netscape Communicator

Uploading files with Netscape Communicator is quite different from using the WS_FTP program. To access your FTP server, you need to type in the user name, password, and FTP address into the Web browser the same way you would type in the address of a Web site. The proper format to use is ftp://username:password@ftp.whatever.com/. If you do not include your password, you will be prompted for it.

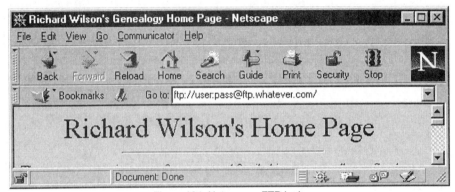

Figure 164: Netscape - FTP login

For my Earthlink account, my username is "richardw," my password is "******," and "ftp-www.earthlink.net" is the location of my FTP site. So, if I put **ftp://richardw:******@ftp-www.earthlink.net/** into the address bar of the Netscape browser and press the <ENTER> key, I will logon to that FTP site (see Figure 164).

You can also login to an anonymous account on an FTP server. Simply use an FTP URL such as **ftp://ftp.whatever.com**.

Once you have accessed the FTP site, you can change directories by clicking on the underlined folders. In this example, the directory I want to go to is "webdocs," so I click on it and change to that directory (see Figure 165).

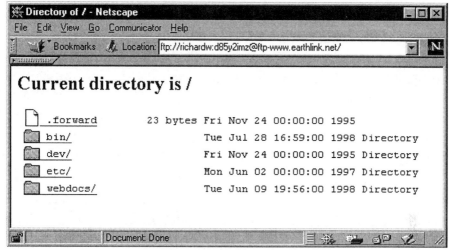

Figure 165: Netscape - FTP directory listing

If a transfer is interrupted, Navigator cannot resume the download or upload. You have to start the transfer again. Also, there are other limitations such as removing or renaming files on the FTP server. If you need any of these features, you may want to use a dedicated FTP program instead.

Drag-and-drop is supported on most operating systems. You can download files by dragging them out of an FTP window, or upload files by dragging them into an FTP window (from Explorer or File Manager). If you are not able to drag files into an FTP window, select "Upload File" from the "File" pull-down menu. Go to the directory where the file you want to upload is located.

Uploading Your Web Pages With Fetch

Fetch is a Macintosh FTP program. The latest version is 3.03. It is available at **ftp://ftp.dartmouth.edu/pub/mac/Fetch_3.0.3.hqx**. Shareware registration cost is $25.00 (US).

Here are the steps for uploading your files with Fetch:

1. Connect to the Internet.

2. Start the Fetch program by clicking on its icon.

3. In the Host area of the window that pops up, type *ftp.yourprovider.com* (this is the destination address your Web space provider gave you).

4. Fill in the User ID and Password spaces with the information e-mailed to you when you signed up with your provider.

5. Click on the "OK" button.

6. A new window will open (see Figure 166).

7. Choose "Put File".

8. A Finder menu will appear. Select your Web page file, click Open and then select "OK" to upload the file.

9. Repeat this process for additional pages and image files.

Remember: Your home page must be named *index.html*. HTML files should be uploaded as Text, and images should be uploaded as Raw Data.

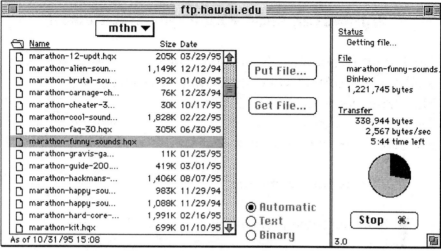

Figure 166: Fetch - main program screen

Checking Your Uploaded Web Pages

Once your Web pages are on the Internet, you need to verify them again. Web pages that appeared to look correct on your computer may not work properly on the Internet server. There are programs available that allow you to check the HTML coding on your Web pages. You can find these programs listed under "HTML Validators" in *Chapter 7*, starting on page 242.

Visit every Web page you have uploaded to be sure they all operate correctly. Follow every external and internal link on your pages to be sure they operate as you have designed them. You might have links that point to locations on your hard drive, rather than on the Internet.

Have others check your Web pages. This is a great way to make sure your Web pages will look okay on computers with different graphic displays and with different Web browsers. Remember, different Web browsers will display your pages differently than your browser does.

Web Sites Where You Can Learn More

Chapter 7

Shareware Software Sites

I mention many software programs and sites in this section, though there are many more programs available that are not listed here. If you are interested in a program that is not mentioned in this book, check one of the following shareware sites.

Download.com:
http://www.download.com/

CNET's Web site of PC software which is available for downloading. You can search for software by category in its up-to-date database of more than 15,000 files. You'll also find reviews, top picks, and in-depth coverage of software. They also have a link to software for the Macintosh computer.

Shareware.com:
http://www.shareware.com/

Another CNET site of more than 250,000 shareware software programs. They also have a searchable database of software titles.

Tucows:
http://www.tucows.com/

For a great Internet software library, check out the Tucows site. They have thousands of the world's best Internet software applications and games for your personal computer. They have a great 5-cow rating system for all of their software.

Advertising Sites

Add It!:
http://www.liquidimaging.com/liqimg/submit/

Use Add it! to advertise your Web site's URL on many of the popular search engines absolutely free.

Add Me!:
http://www.addme.com/

At this Web site, you can submit your Web site to 34 of the popular search engines for free.

Broadcaster:
http://www.broadcaster.co.uk/

At this Web site, you can submit your site to the top search engines and information resources on the Web and much more.

FreeLinks:
http://www.freelinks.com/

FreeLinks is a guide to free web site promotions, search engines and directories, and webmaster tools and resources.

Kwik-Submit:
http://www.simple123.com/kse2opt.html

A **paid** service. You can add your site listing to as many as 370 of the top search engines and Web page listings with one form, at one time, for $29.95.

NetAnnounce Free:
http://softwaresolutions.net/netsubmitter/

You can quickly get your site listed with 20 of the Internet's most popular search engines and directories for free. They also offer submissions to more sites for a fee.

Net Submitter Professional:
http://softwaresolutions.net/netsubmitter/

Net Submitter Professional provides fully automated submission of unlimited URLs to a growing list of over 440 search engines, directories, newsgroups, and link listings. In addition, semi-automated support is provided for hundreds of other submission sites. Registration **fee** is $99.95 (US).

Search & Submit:
http://www.212.net/search/a-search.htm

A link to many search engines. You can manually submit information to these search engines for no cost.

Submissions.com:
http://www.submissions.com/

Use this automated submission software to "instantly" submit your Web site to over 800 search engines. The cost of this software is quite high, $30.00 (US) for one month to $130.00 (US) for one year.

Submit it! Free:
http://siteowner.linkexchange.com/Free.cfm

Submit It! Free is a free service for companies and individuals wishing to promote their own Web sites. Use Submit It! Free to quickly, accurately, and easily submit your URL to over 20 search engines and directories at one time for no charge.

WebStep Top 100:
http://www.mmgco.com/top100.html

Links to 100 of the top Web search engines. The search engines are ranked on a one to four star rating.

TrafficBoost:
http://trafficboost.com/?Goldberg

Commercial service that submits your site to 530 search engines and directories. The **fee** for this service is $49.00 (US).

Counters and Guest Books

Extreme Tracker:
http://www4.icount.com/cgi/chan.cgi

Extreme is a new entry into the ever growing free counter arena. It is comprehensive and reliable and it doesn't show advertisements on your page, just a little Extreme Counter logo. It has many very good statistics for you to keep track of things. One excellent feature is its page referral statistics which provide you with details of where your hits are coming from.

Guestbook*Star:
http://www.webgenie.com/Software/Guestar/

Guestbook*Star is a shareware guestbook creator by Web Genie. It allows you to create a guestbook instantly without any programming or CGI knowledge. Registration cost for this program is $29.00 (US).

Guestbook Depot:
http://www.guestbookdepot.com/

This is another free guest book site. This guest book has many options you have control over.

GuestWorld:
http://www.Lpage.com/

You can get a free guest book at GuestWorld. They provide guest books for over a half million Web site owners around the world.

JCount Free Counter Creation Page:
http://www.jcount.com/

J-Count is nice looking and easy to use. It includes some fairly simple statistics, such as hits per day and per week, and the ability to change the counter style even after registering. It is completely free if you do not mind the advertisements.

PIN's Guide to free Web counters:
http://members.tripod.com/~tammytrout/cindex.htm

This site has a rating system for all the free counters on the Internet. Included are reviews and a section for pay counters. This site should be helpful in choosing the best counter for your requirements.

PR-Tracker's FREE Webpage Hit Counter:
http://www.prtracker.com/freecounter.html

This is a simple hit counter designed to help you easily track hits on a single Web page or multiple Web pages. It is a free tracker, if you do not mind a large banner ad type of counter.

WebSideStory:
http://www.hitbox.com/wc/world.html

A very popular tracker, which is usually used in conjunction with another counter. It doesn't display the number of hits on your page, just a little animated button. It has a large set of statistics and the option to join the Web Side Story top 1,000 list. This list is a good way to get yourself more hits, if your page is popular enough to be listed. To view your statistics, you need to use the URL they provide. If your site is not accessed in a 24-hour period, however, it will not be listed in the top 1000, causing you to have to re-register (your statistics and count continue to work, though).

FTP Programs

Anarchie Pro 3.5:
http://www.stairways.com/anarchie/

Anarchie Pro 3.5 is an FTP program for the Macintosh. During Anarchie's six year evolution, it has met the needs of Macintosh Internet users in many areas. It has recently been nominated for the Macworld 1998 Editors' Choice Award for Best Internet Client Software, the most prestigious award available. It has many uses and features without becoming cluttered and hard to use due to its elegant and very "Macintosh" interface.

Bulletproof FTP:
http://www.bpftp.com/

Bulletproof FTP is a shareware FTP program with an intuitive, drag-and-drop interface and some very nice features. It allows you to download or upload files in any order from any directory on an FTP site. If your Internet connection is lost in the middle of the transfer, it will automatically reconnect and resume right where it left off. Registration is $29.95 (US).

Cute FTP:
http://www.cuteftp.com/

This FTP program has drag and drop capabilities, bookmarks, auto rename scheme and resume download. They also offer a powerful macro that records your activities so you can play back specific transfers and automate your work. It includes a directory compare feature and remote file editing for HTML documents. It has an Internet Explorer style toolbar. The registration price is $34.95 (US).

Fetch:
http://www.dartmouth.edu/pages/softdev/fetch.html

Fetch is an excellent Macintosh FTP program. It is very fast and easy to use. It allows you to bookmark your favorite sites, upload and download files in groups, and decompress files on the fly. Registration is $25.00 (US).

FTP Control Pro:
http://www.ftpcontrol.com

This is an FTP program with functions that extend far beyond the usual FTP programs. Control Pro supports the automation of scheduled file transfers (uploading and downloading), and has the option to download in the background so you can continue to surf other FTP sites. Control Pro can also resume an aborted transfer where it left off, saving you valuable time and money. Registration is $29.00 (US).

Transmit:
http://www.panic.com/transmit/download.html

An FTP program for the Macintosh. Features include: resumable downloads, folder/file synchronization, MacBinary III encoding, and more. Requires a Macintosh with System 7.5 or later.

WS_FTP:
http://www.ipswitch.com/Products/WS_FTP/

WS_FTP LE is a freeware FTP program. They also make WS_FTP Pro, a shareware program. This is an easy-to-use application that allows remote file editing and very easy file moves. Registration price of WS_FTP Pro is $37.50 (US).

Genealogy to HTML Converters

AHN Program:
http://homepages.munich.netsurf.de/Helmut.Braess/pgrAhne.htm

A shareware program that can show genealogical data, stored in a GEDCOM file, as a family tree or ancestor list. It uses Java Script to operate. The charts can be shown in two formats, list style or graph style. Use of the program is free. To make the program operate on your Web site you need to get a file from the program's author.

Ancestral Quest:
http://www.ancquest.com/

A commercial genealogy software program. See the program description starting on page 68.

Family Origins:
http://www.parsonstech.com/software/fowin7.html

A commercial genealogy software program. See the program description on page 72.

Family Tree Maker:
http://www.familytreemaker.com/ftmvers.html

A commercial genealogy software program. See the program description on page 77.

GED Browser:
http://www.misbach.org/

A shareware program for converting your genealogy to HTML. The current version is 1.1 dated November 30, 1998. It can display both descendants and ancestors in one chart, giving virtually all the information found on a family group sheet. It creates a "Site Map" view of your genealogy showing your entire genealogical tree in a way that graphically depicts the shape of your tree, with every individual represented and linked to their individual pedigree chart. Registration fee is $10.00.

GED2HTM:
http://table.jps.net/~johns1/#gedpaf

A shareware conversion program . See program description on page 82. Registration cost is $5.00 (US) but is not required.

GED2HTML:
http://www.gendex.com/ged2html/

A full-featured shareware conversion program. See the description of this program on page 87. Registration cost for this program is $20.00 (US) and is good for updates for one year from the registration date.

GED2Web:
http://www.oramwt.demon.co.uk/GED2WEB/ged2web.htm

Ged2web is shareware program for generating a set of Web pages from a GEDCOM file. The current version is 2.64, dated February 11, 1999. The registration fee is free for a limited time.

GED2WWW:
http://pw2.netcom.com/~lhoward/ged2www.html

A freeware conversion program. See the program description starting on page 94.

GEDHTREE:
http://www.users.uswest.net/~gwel/gedhtree.htm

A shareware conversion program written by E. Gary Welker. The current version is 1.02a, dated March 12, 1999. This program can process a GEDCOM file to generate an ancestor tree, family group sheets and index pages in HTML format. Registration is $14.95 (US).

GEDPage:
http://www.frontiernet.net/~rjacob/gedpage.htm

A full-featured shareware conversion program . The author listens to suggestions and is willing to make modifications to the program. See the program description starting on page 98. Registration is $10 (US).

GEDTable:
http://www.frontiernet.net/~rjacob/gedpage.htm

A shareware conversion program that simply reads a GEDCOM File and then creates Web pages from the data in that file. It presents the data in a table format. You need to be aware that these GEDTable The Web pages it creates are currently only visible with IE4 or IE5. The Web pages use an ActiveX control and Internet Explorer is the only browser that currently supports it. Registration is free, they even offer free Web space to put your files on their server.

GenDesigner:
http://www.gendesigner.com/

This program can create and edit Web pages from your family data. You may include additional text and pictures for each person as well as distribute your genealogical tree on the Internet. Registration is $29.95 (US).

HTMLGenie:
http://www.geneaware.com/software/index.html

HTMLGenie is a commercial Web publishing tool that allows the user to create instant HTML pages from a GEDCOM file. There is no editing to be done after the files are produced. Colors and font sizes can be selected before generating the HTML files. In addition, you can add your own background image, or your own page banner image or title. HTMLGenie outputs data in any of the following formats: descendancy list, modified register, family detail records, and ahnentafel list. It also has a privacy selection so you can establish a cutoff year. Any persons born after that year will not have any dates associated with their data. This applies to all output formats. Registration cost is $29.95 (US).

Indexed GEDCOM Method (IGM):
http://www.rootsweb.com/~gumby/igm.html

This program creates HTML index files from your GEDCOM file. When someone finds a person they want to know more about, they can request more information. The HTML index instructs the Web Server to run the IGMGet program, which opens the GEDCOM file and goes directly to the person indicated. It then loads all of the information for that person and his/her family, generates an HTML file, and sends it back to the user. This program requires you to have access to your server's CGI directory.

Kinship Archivist:
http://www.frugal.com/~evjendan/ancestry.html/

A shareware genealogy program that can create HTML files. You can enter your data into the program, or import it as a GEDCOM file. Each family member will have their own Web page, and genealogical information is linked between the Web pages. The registration cost is $20.00 (US).

Legacy:
http://www.legacyfamilytree.com/

A full-featured commercial genealogy program. See the program description starting on page 110.

Sparrowhawk:
http://www.tjp.washington.edu/bdm/genealogy/sparrowhawk.html

Sparrowhawk is a shareware GEDCOM-to-HTML conversion program for the Macintosh. It is based on version 2.5a of Gene Stark's GED2HTML program for Windows and UNIX. Sparrowhawk will create a set of linked HTML documents from the genealogical information contained in a GEDCOM file. The output from Sparrowhawk is essentially identical to the output of GED2HTML 2.5. Single user registration is $20.00 (US).

uFTi:
http://www.ufti.demon.co.uk/homepage.htm

uFTi is a freeware program that converts genealogical data from a GEDCOM file. The data is stored in a relational database that can be exported to the World Wide Web for publishing your family history on the Internet. uFTi is being developed in line with the GENWEB™

project (not the USGenWeb Project), which is linking pages of genealogical research using the Internet. This program is available in English, Swedish, German, and Dutch.

Ultimate Family Tree:
http://www.uftree.com/

A commercial genealogy program. See the program description starting on page 127.

Webbit:
http://www.compuology.com/genfiles/webbit14.zip

A freeware conversion program. See its program description starting on page 133.

webGED: Progenitor 2.0:
http://www.access.digex.net/~giammot/webged/

This shareware program accepts a standard GEDCOM file as input and produces the complete set of files for a self-contained WWW site. The user can then upload these files to his/her Internet Service Provider's server to have the information immediately available on the Internet. Registration cost is $20.00 (US).

Win-Family:
http://www.jamodat.dk/

A shareware genealogy program. This program can create Web pages out of your genealogical data. Registration fee is $50.00 (US).

Programs to Remove Living Information

GEDClean:
http://www.raynorshyn.com/gedclean/

This freeware program works with a GEDCOM file to remove information about living persons. See the program description on page 51. There is no cost to register this program.

GEDLiving:
http://www.rootsweb.com/~gumby/ged.html

This shareware program works to remove the data about living individuals in a GEDCOM file.

GEDPrivy:
http://members.aol.com/gedprivy/

This shareware program works with a GEDCOM file to remove information about living persons. See the program description on page 56 of this book. Registration cost is $10 (US).

Res Privata:
http://www.ozemail.com.au/~naibor/rpriv.html

Res Privata is a shareware program you can use to filter out the details for living individuals in your original GEDCOM file. It creates a new GEDCOM file ready for sharing with other genealogists or publishing on the Internet. See a description of this program starting on page 58.

Graphics for Your Web Pages

Animate Page:
http://www.vrl.com/

This page is part of the VRL Imaging Machine. You can use it to create a single animated GIF file from a series of TIFF, GIF, PNM, HDF, PS, or MIFF files.

Animations and Graphics For Your Website:
http://www.bellsnwhistles.com/graphics.html

These pages have been put together in order to make your Web page design a little easier. In the non-animated section, it contains over 200 horizontal rules, about 150 different bullets, many icons, and over 250 original background images. In the animated section, you will find well over 700 horizontal rules, bullets, icons, fire animations, construction icons, globes, signs, stars, e-mail icons and arrows. All of the animations on this site have been reduced to their smallest possible byte size. There are a few, however, that are kept in a larger size because of their value to specialized interests. It is their aim to supply you with animations which will not appreciably slow the load time for your site.

Clip Art Connection:
http://www.ist.net/clipart/index.html

A Web site with links to thousands of graphics for your Web pages.

Creating Transparent GIF images using LView Pro:
http://www.iconbazaar.com/tutorials/

This is a tutorial by Randy Ralph on how to convert your GIF images to transparent GIF images.

GraphicConverter:
http://www.lemkesoft.de/

A Macintosh shareware program for Web builders and graphic picture handlers. GraphicConverter can open and convert most graphic file types. Registration cost $35.00 (US).

Graphic Workshop:
http://www.mindworkshop.com/alchemy/gwspro.html

Graphic Workshop is an image utility that can view and convert many different image formats.

LView Pro:
http://www.lview.com/

A comprehensive shareware graphics package that enables you to create images from scratch or edit existing image files. The program now supports Twain-compatible devices (such as scanners and frame-grabber cards), and its fresh, intuitive interface has been optimized for Windows 95/98/NT. Along with the usual assortment of file operations (such as copy, move, delete, and rename), LView Pro features extensive cataloging options, slide shows, format conversion operations, and support for image animation. It also offers transparency, painting tools, color matching, special effects, and the ability to store thumbnail images with text descriptions. The registration cost for this program is $40.00 (US).

MAS Media Utilities:
http://www.pmace.com/

MAS Media Utilities offers a solution to all multimedia and image processing needs in a single Windows application. It streamlines one of the most frustrating aspects of multimedia and Web authoring: finding, previewing, re-formatting and converting existing animations and images. The registration fee for this program is $99.00 (US).

Paint Shop Pro:
http://www.jasc.com/

An excellent shareware graphics program which supports several image formats, screen capturing, batch image format conversion, has an integrated image browser, and complete photo retouching. New features include complete layer support, Picture Tube brushes, separations, and pressure-sensitive tablet support. It also has enhancements to Paint Shop Pro's flexible painting and retouching brushes, adjustable cropping and selection tools, and image enhancements. Registration cost is $69.00 (US).

Transparent GIF Backgrounds:
http://jasc.com/transtip.html

A tutorial by Jasc Software. How to create transparent GIF images using Paint Shop Pro, version 3.11 or newer.

HTML Editors

1-4-All:
http://www.mmsoftware.com/14All/

This shareware HTML editor software has a unique CodeQuick feature, a fully integrated publishing wizard, an internal HTML viewer and image viewer, predefined Javascripts, instant color coding (even with large files), project management, template support, spell checker, and much more. The program will run in either the English or German languages. Registration cost is $30.00 (US).

Arachnophilia:
http://www.arachnoid.com/arachnophilia/

A "CareWare" (it is not about money, it is about caring) HTML editor and workshop. With it, you can import fully formatted text, tables, and outlines then watch as they are converted into HTML code complete with colors, fonts, and styles. This program supports: CGI, Frames, Java, Javascript, and C++ development. Arachnophilia even has an FTP client built-in to automatically update your Web site.

Homesite:
http://www.allaire.com/products/homesite/index.cfm

A shareware editor program that includes fully customizable color coding, built-in HTML 3.0-compliant Web browser, multi-file search and replace, an Explorer-style directory view for easy access to HTML documents, user-defined tool buttons, rulers, block indenting, and more. Registration cost is $79.00 (US).

HotDog Express:
http://www.sausage.com/

HotDog Express is a shareware program that lets you create and upload a Web page in four simple steps without knowing any HTML. Even people who are novices on the Web can use HotDog Express and make a Web-page in just five minutes. You can let HotDog Express automatically upload to your ISP to publish your genealogy on the Internet. Registration cost is $49.95 (US).

Hot Dog Professional Web Editor:
http://www.sausage.com/

One of the best HTML editors available (the one I use). The interface is attractive, powerful, configurable, and intuitive. You can set up buttons on the toolbars to do almost anything you want. It has a built in HTML validator and a spell checker. Registration cost is $149.95 (US).

NoteTab HTML Editor:
http://www.notetab.com/

This is a shareware text and HTML editor for Windows 95, 98, and NT4. It is user friendly and feature rich with many innovative productivity tools. This editor is capable of handling extremely large files, supports variable-pitch fonts and works well with non-roman alphabets such as Chinese, Hebrew, etc. Registration is $19.95 (US).

Visual Page:
http://www.symantec.com/vpagemac/guide/overview.html

Symantec Visual Page for the Macintosh is fast, robust, and easy to use. It is a WYSIWYG Web page editor. You can bring dynamic and colorful Web pages to life, without having to learn the Internet's HTML language.

Web Scrapbook:
http://www.webprecinct.com/WebScrapbook/Introduction.htm

This is an easy to use freeware HTML program for creating your own Web pages. No HTML knowledge is required, just let their Internet Imp show how to make great looking Web pages in a matter of minutes.

Web Weaver 98:
http://www.mcwebsoftware.com/webweav.html

Web Weaver 98 is a shareware HTML editor that makes creating Web pages quick and easy. Good for beginners, as well as advanced users of HTML, it features colored HTML codes for easier editing and wizards for advanced HTML elements such as frames, tables, and forms. It has tool bars, dialog boxes, hypertext, inline images, anchors and lists, context-sensitive help, and more. It supports all HTML 2 and 3.2 tags, as well as most Netscape and Internet Explorer extensions. Preview your work-in-progress with the click of a button. Registration price is just $25.00 (US).

HTML and Web Training

A Beginner's Guide to HTML:
http://www.ncsa.uiuc.edu/General/Internet/WWW/HTMLPrimer.html

Many people use this guide as a starting point to understanding the hypertext markup language (HTML) used on the World Wide Web. It is an introduction and does not pretend to offer instructions on every aspect of HTML. Links to additional Web-based resources about HTML and other related aspects of preparing files are provided at the end of the guide.

Bare Bones Guide to HTML:
http://werbach.com/barebones/

The Bare Bones Guide to HTML lists every official HTML tag in common usage, including the Netscape extensions. Version 3.0 of the Guide conforms to the HTML 3.2 specification. They are currently working on a version based on the public draft of HTML 4.0.

Copyright Information:
http://www.rootsweb.com/~usgenweb/copyrite.txt

This Web page gives information about when works pass into the public domain.

Cyndi's Genealogy Home Page Construction Kit:
http://www.cyndislist.com/construc.htm

Designed to be a quick start guide for people to use when creating and designing their own genealogy Web page, maintained by Cyndi Howells. Creating a Web page of your own isn't as hard as you might think it is.

Freedback.com:
http://Freedback.com/?ff/

This Web site offers you free feedback forms you can add to your Web pages. They allow you to create an easy way to get feedback from visitors without having to design your own forms.

HTML Bad Style Page:
http://www.earth.com/bad-style/

This page is designed to serve as an educational tool for users learning HTML. This collection is in no way comprehensive, just some of the more common problems that are seen.

How to Set Up and Maintain a Web Site:
http://www.genome.wi.mit.edu/WWW/tools/index.html

This Web site contains directories with software and other tools that are useful in creating and maintaining a Web site

HTML Specifications:
http://www.w3.org/MarkUp/

The World Wide Web Consortium (W3C) HTML page. This page has links to the current HTML standard (4.0) as well as links to older and futures versions.

HTML Reference Library:
http://subnet.virtual-pc.com/~le387818/

This site is devoted to providing information about HTML. This reference library is a Windows HLP file that details (with numerous screenshots and examples) all of the currently supported HTML elements. As such, it is the ideal companion for anybody involved in HTML development and, best of all, it is absolutely free.

HTML Vocabulary:
http://www.calles.pp.se/nisseb/

A Macintosh shareware program. It is a handy reference to the HyperText Markup Language, available when you need it and updated frequently. HTML Vocabulary contains the most well-used HTML codes including special characters, frames, tables, forms, stylesheets, and Netscape Navigator and Internet Explorer additions. Registration cost is $5.00 (US).

Learning Beginning & Advanced HTML:
http://www.geocities.com/Heartland/Valley/2248/tips.html

This Web site is set up with links to all the help you need to create your very own Web pages.

Library of Congress HTML Guide:
http://lcweb.loc.gov/global/internet/html.html

This Web site is set up with links to tutorials on all aspects of Web page creation.

Meta Tag Generator:
http://www.cozycabin.com/metatags.html

This Web site will create the codes for Meta tags for your Web pages. You simply input the information and click on a button and it will generate the proper Meta tag code for you.

US Patient and Trademark Office:
http://www.uspto.gov/

This Web site has information and forms for patients and trademarks.

WebCom HTML Guide:
http://www.webcom.com/html/tutor/

This Web site has tutorials on all aspects of Web page creation.

Web Authoring FAQ:
http://www.htmlhelp.com/faq/html/all.html

This is a list of frequently asked questions maintained by the Web Design Group.

Web Pages That Suck:
http://www.webpagesthatsuck.com/

This site provides links to Web sites with very bad designs, so you can learn what you shouldn't do when you create Web pages.

Web Site Development and Internet Education:
http://www.schoolofwebdesign.com/

This site provides HTML lessons, useful resources, and links to worthy sites to help you grow in your Web site creation, and do it all for free.

HTML Validators

CSE 3310 HTML Validator:
http://htmlvalidator.com/

A very nice and easy-to-use shareware HTML validator. You can drag and drop your HTML documents to this program and it returns a very thorough list of any errors it finds in the HTML codes–in plain English. It even tells you exactly which tags are causing the error (i.e., if you have overlapping tags, the program will tell you exactly which ones are overlapping, etc.). Registration is $24.95 (US).

Doctor HTML:
http://www2.imagiware.com/RxHTMLpro/

Doctor HTML is a commercial online Web page analysis tool which retrieves an HTML page and reports any problems it finds on that page. The primary focus of this tool is to provide a clear, easy-to-use report of information that is relevant for improving your Web page. This is a good way to check your pages once you upload them to the Internet. Cost is $50.00 for 100 reports. They do offer you a limited guest access to try their program.

Linkbot Pro:
http://www.tetranetsoftware.com/linkbot-info.htm

A powerful site management tool for Webmasters. Linkbot makes it easy to visualize the structure of your site, find broken links, missing titles, and other problems that plague Webmasters. The output of Linkbot's analysis can be exported to HTML or a delimited file. Registration cost after 30-day trial is $295.00 (US).

LinkCop:
http://linkcop.com

A useful shareware link validation utility, that thoroughly checks your Website's internal links, external links, and even your CGI programs. You can also configure the program to run at scheduled times. When it performs its routine link check up, the program automatically e-mails a complete diagnostic to a specified recipient (such as yourself). Registration fee is $34.95.

W3C HTML Validation Service:
http://validator.w3.org/

This is an easy-to-use HTML validation service based on an SGML parser. It checks HTML documents for compliance with W3C HTML Recommendations and other HTML standards.

Utility Programs

Coollist:
http://www.coollist.com/

Coollist is a Web-based system that allows users to create free mailing lists on the Coollist server. The Coollist system is easy to use and is accessible from anywhere in the world. Create your own surname or geographic mail list.

DB-HTML Converter Pro:
http://www.primasoft.com/dbhtmlp.htm

This is a shareware HTML database utility that creates Web pages from popular formats such as MSSQL, FoxPro, MS Access, DB2, Informix, Oracle, Sybase, and others. Registration fee is $103.00 US.

GEDCOM Utility Files:
http://www.rootsweb.com/~gumby/ged.html

Various programs designed to operate with GEDCOM files, such as GEDSplit.exe - a program to split any GEDCOM file in useful ways, Analyze.exe - a program to display the unconnected individuals in any GEDCOM file, GEDPlace.exe - a program that allows editing of places in a GEDCOM file, and more.

HTML PowerTools:
http://www.tali.com/indexo.html

These tools allow the HTML developer to create better Web pages in less time. All are Windows 3.x or Windows 95/98/NT versions. You can ensure that your HTML is perfect for any or all browsers, verify that all your links are valid, weed out obsolete files from your site, make sure that the major search engines correctly list your Web site, search and replace an entire Web site with unique HTML-aware facilities, automatically fix all mismatched tag pairs, and convert any number of Web pages to formatted text files with one click. Cost is $59.95 (US).

HTML Rename!:
http://www.visiontec.com/rename/

A shareware program for Macintosh or Windows that can help you do mass file renames to fit different operating systems. In other words, if you need to rename all your files from *name.html* to *name.htm*, or *name.htm* to *longfilename.html*, this program can do it. *HTML Rename!* will quickly and easily convert all the filenames, as well as fixing all the references to the renamed files within the files. Easy to use, fast, and powerful. Registration cost is $20.00 (US).

Infolink:
http://www.biggbyte.com/

This shareware utility makes it easy for you to check the links on your Web pages. You simply give it the location of an HTML file on the Internet, then it searches out the links and lets you know which are working and which are not. Registration cost is $49.95 (US).

NetMind:
http://www.netmind.com/

You can register at this Web site to be notified when any Web pages you are interested in are changed. They will monitor the Web pages and notify you anytime the pages are updated.

P.S.Mail:

http://www.compsol.net/users/bplude/nocgi.htm

A shareware program that takes e-mail sent from a Web page form and converts it into a workable database. Record fields are then editable and searchable. Users can design a return e-mail from within the program. You can custom design your converter with up to seven visitor questions. You can get reports to track people that visit your site. All of this can be done without accessing the cgi-bin directory located on your server. Registration cost is not yet determined.

Web Browsers

HotJava:
http://java.sun.com/products/hotjava/

HotJava is a full-featured, lightweight Web browser with a highly customizable user interface. It is built on the HotJava code base, which provides a secure, platform-independent, scalable, and customizable base for building Web-aware applications and suites that are 100% pure Java.

Internet Explorer:
http://www.microsoft.com/windows/ie/download/windows.htm

Microsoft's download site for their Internet Explorer Web browser.

NCSA Mosaic:
http://www.ncsa.uiuc.edu/SDG/Software/mosaic-w/

This Internet browser was developed at the National Center for Supercomputing Applications (NCSA) at the University of Illinois. NCSA Mosaic software is copyrighted by The Board of Trustees of the University of Illinois (UI). This Web browser is still under major development and upgrades.

NetCruiser:
http://www.netcom.com/netcom/netcrz.html

NetCruiser is an older Web browser designed to help you move easily through the Internet. You can browse the World Wide Web, connect to other computers on the Internet (via Telnet and FTP), or read and write messages using e-mail or NetNews.

Netscape Communicator:
http://home.netscape.com/download/

Software download site for Netscape Navigator and Netscape Communicator.

Opera:
http://operasoftware.com/

Opera is a shareware Web browser supporting CSS, Java (through the Sun Java plug-in), Java-Script SSL, and TLS. This program is small and compact. Opera uses multiple windows to navigate around the Internet, each one with its own history and home-page settings. Because of its small size, Opera is ideal for speed surfers (faster page loading), visually challenged users (keyboard navigation), and those with older PCs (386). Opera also includes a News reader and simple mail support. Opera is compatible with most Netscape plug-ins. Registration cost is $35.00 (US).

Web Design Aids

100 Top Web Building Sites:
http://www.bcpl.lib.md.us/~owl/planet/100topwebsites.html

Everyone knows what goes into making a great Web page: Sharp graphics, a nice layout, and an interesting but usable background. But what is a lot harder is knowing where you'll find it. This site contains sorted links with the best graphics, backgrounds, HTML editors, and tutorials that are on the Web for free.

Richard's Web Page Comparison Site:
http://www.compuology.com/richard/compare.htm

This Web site displays genealogical data on Web pages created by a variety of different commercial and shareware programs. These Web pages were created by Richard S. Wilson.

So, You Want to Make a Web Page!:
http://junior.apk.net/~jbarta/tutor/makapage/index.html

This tutorial is one in a series of WebTutor tutorials. It is also available for downloading as a self-extracting zip file. Just a note—this tutorial is geared towards those using Windows 95/98 and is biased towards Netscape; however, most of it should work just fine for those using Internet Explorer or other operating systems.

Transforming your GEDCOM Files into Web Pages:
http://www.oz.net/~markhow/writing/gedcom.htm

This article was written by Mark Howells. It covers various ways to create Web pages from your genealogical data.

Various Genealogy Presentation Forms:
http://www.pinn.net/~knightma/

This Web site displays genealogical data on Web pages created by a variety of different programs. These Web pages were created by Mark A. Knight.

Web Site Design Guide:
http://www.geocities.com/Athens/4204/

This site is full of information and links that are related to designing a Web site. Whether you're interested in creating a home page, a multiple page Web site, or just want to spice up an existing page or site, then this is a good place for you to check out.

Web Space Providers

Angelfire:
http://www.angelfire.com/

They offer free Web space for your genealogy.

Compuology:
http://www.compuology.com/webpub/

I just had to mention this one <G>. They offer free Web space for Genealogical societies and USGenWeb sites. They offer low-cost Web space for other personal sites.

Fortune City:
http://www.fortunecity.com/

They offer you a free e-mail address and twenty megabytes of Web space for free.

Free Web Space:
http://serge.simplenet.com/design.html

Promoteam Limited offers free e-mail, free Web space, and free Web advertising on search engines.

Geocities:
http://www.geocities.com/join/freehp.html

They offer free Web space. They display a floating advertizing banner any time someone accesses one of their free Web sites.

Interspeed Network:
http://www.interspeed.net/

They offer unlimited storage, traffic, and e-mail forwarding. They charge $9.95 a month for Web space.

MyFamily.com:
http://www.MyFamily.com/

You can set up a free private Web area for your family. Use the Web space to share photos, video clips, sound files, your genealogy and a group calendar for your family.

RootsWeb:
http://www.rootsweb.com/

They offer free Web space for Genealogical societies and USGenWeb sites. They offer low-cost Web space for other personal sites.

Tripod:
http://homepager.tripod.com/

Tripod offers free disk space as a benefit of membership. They display a floating advertizing banner any time someone accesses one of their free Web sites.

WebProvider.com - Free Web Space:
http://www.webprovider.com/

They offer five megabytes of free Web space. They also offer free a virtual Web hosting service, your only cost is InterNIC's yearly domain registration fee for your own personal domain name.

Free/Low-cost Advertising for Your Web Site

Chapter 8

Traditional Media

Once you have created a great Web site, you want to advertise it so people will know about it. There are many different ways of making your presence known on the Internet. The first thing to do is add your URL to your letterhead and business cards. Anywhere you have an address listed, make sure your URL is included.

Once your site is up and running, you should write a press release with information about your site and what it has to offer. Do not forget to include the URL address. Send your press release out to various publications that are willing to list Web sites. Local newspapers love to hear news of an exciting or unique Web site offered on the Internet. Do not forget genealogy publications - both paper and Internet. Encourage them to review your site in their publication.

Richard Says:

Genealogical Societies are always looking for articles for their newsletters. These are great places to send information about your site. Also, most newsletters also include a "Web sites" section in them.

Search Engines and Indexes

You'll definitely want to have your URL added to some of the various catalogs of Web pages archived on the Internet. Search engines and directories are some of the most popular ways people locate information on the Web. Before you submit your URL, however, you should be aware of a few things.

First of all, you need to understand how the engines and directories rank the Web sites in their databases. Many of them provide an explanation of the method they use, but there are some general rules. Most important are the keywords they use for your site.

The parts of your site that determines its ranking are the title and the META tags (see "Meta Tags" in Chapter 5 starting on page 170). The first few paragraphs on your Web pages are the next most important part.

All search engines use keywords inputted by users to determine which pages people would be most interested in viewing. Each search engine has a different method of determining which pages come up in the results of a keyword search. This method is called "scoring." The pages with the highest scores will be displayed first.

You need to decide what keywords you want to use for your Web site. This is very important. Take some time to jot down all the keywords you can think of. Ask friends, relatives, and other researchers to help. Make sure you include keywords from your most important Web pages, such as your surname pages.

Now that you have your list, decide which ones you'd like to keep and which ones you do not. You will probably just want to start with fifteen of the most likely keywords. You can always come back and add the others later.

All search engines score your page higher if your keywords are in the same order as those that the searcher entered. For example, if a person searches for "Wilson Tennessee genealogy," a site with the words "Isaac Wilson's Tennessee genealogy and family history" will score higher than one with the words "Wilson genealogy in Tennessee."

One method of finding out how to get listed near the top of a search engine list is to do a keyword search in that search engine. Use any keyword you like, but not too general. When the search results come up, take note of the title and description of the very first Web site listed. Click on it to go to their page. Use your browser's "View Source" button to see their HTML codes. Study it carefully. Do they have the keyword repeated numerous times? Do they have keywords listed somewhere in the title? Look for the <META> tags in their <HEAD> section. These cannot be seen by just by viewing the page with your Web browser. You need to look at the source code.

Once you register your site with a search engine, it will "read" your Web pages and automatically store words from your Web site in its database. When someone does a keyword search, the engine does not have to search the entire Web, only its database. The advantage to this is speed. The disadvantage is that once your site is registered, any changes you make are not included in the search engine's database. You must resubmit your pages so that it again reads your Web pages into its database, which could take anywhere from a day to a month.

Putting keywords in the title of your Web page is very important. Your page will score higher if you have those keywords in your title. Make sure the text that follows your title is descriptive of your Web site, and also contains your keywords. Both the title and the description should be short and to the point. There are usually limits to the length of titles and descriptions.

Below is a list of some of the best places to submit your URL at this time. Each has a different process to get your information added to their database. When you visit each site, you can find out what is required to get your URLs included on that list by choosing the "Add URL," or "Add A Page" option, etc. Sometimes you have to search around their site for the link. See Figure 167 for an example from the Alta Vista search engine.

Alta Vista	**(http://www.altavista.digital.com/)**
Excite	**(http://www.excite.com/)**
HotBot	**(http://www.hotbot.com/)**
InfoSeek	**(http://www.infoseek.com/)**
Lycos	**(http://www.lycos.com/)**
WebCrawler	**(http://www.WebCrawler.com/)**
Yahoo!	**(http://www.yahoo.com/)**

Figure 167: Alta Vista - adding URLs

Another method of adding your URL to search engines or directories is by using a Web page submission site, such as "Submit It!" (**http://siteowner.linkexchange.com/Free.cfm**). Submit It! is a free service that allows you to submit your URL to over twenty search engines at one time.

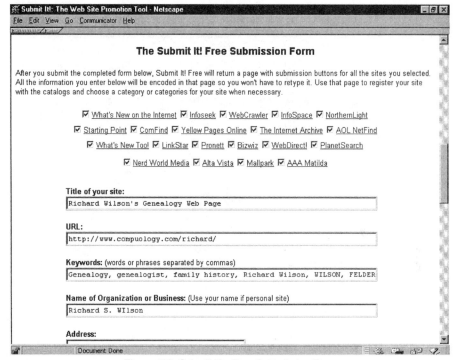

Figure 168: Submit It! - Free Submission Form

When you use Submit It!, you simply fill out a questionnaire and it does most of the work for you. You can choose which sites it sends your submissions to by selecting the check boxes at the top of the page (see Figure 168).

The Web pages (URL) that you want to make sure you register are your main Web home page, as well as any Web pages you have with surname lists on them. People doing searches only for particular surnames will also find your Web page. When you search for a surname, use the word "surname." when you type in keywords. That way you will find genealogy pages instead of a variety of other pages in which that name appears.

You can find additional services to advertise your Web site in "Advertising Sites" in *Chapter 7,* starting on page 218.

Genealogy Specific Sites

Following is a partial list of some genealogy-related sites where you can register your new Web site.

Cyndi's List on the Internet

Cyndi's List (**http://www.cyndislist.com/**) is very good place to register your new Web page URL. She has a very large site with thousands of links.

GENDEX

If you used a GEDCOM-to-HTML converter that created a gendex file, then an excellent place to have your page indexed is at the Gendex Web site (**http://www.gendex.com/gendex/**). At this site, you can e-mail the Webmaster with information about where to find your page and your *gendex.txt* file. He or she will insert all of the names from your Web pages into their database, along with links back to your page.

I Found It!

I Found It! (**http://www.gensource.com/ifoundit/index.htm**) is a directory of genealogy related sites on the Web. You should submit your new site to them because only genealogy sites are permitted to be indexed.

Internet Family Finder

FamilyFinder (**http://www.familytreemaker.com/ifftop.html**) is a new search engine for finding ancestors on the Internet. It will index every word of your entire genealogy Web site, not just the first paragraphs of each page, as many of the other search engines do.

Web Billboard Advertising

A very popular but expensive method of promoting your site is with "billboard" ads, also called banner advertizing One type is the little rectangular graphics near the top or bottom of a Web page, beckoning you to click on them and go to their site. Then there are those that rotate or change. Your ad may appear to only a percentage of the audience of that site (i.e., every fourth person to logon to that site). This is not as bad as it seems, however, because many of those are repeat visitors who will eventually see it.

If you do not want to pay for billboard advertising, there are some free providers. One of the free banner services is called LinkExchange (**http://www.linkexchange.com/addit/**). They provide you with free banner advertising, as long as you display their banner on your site. The more traffic your page gets, the more banners you have on other people's pages, and the more banners other people have displayed on your pages.

What's New Lists and What's Cool Lists

Many places on the Internet keep "What's New" and/or "What's Cool" lists. Since your Web site is new, you should apply to all the places you can find and try to get on their lists. These lists change often, but are read by large numbers of people.

"What's Really New in WWW Genealogy Pages" is located at **http://www.genhomepage.com/really_new.html.** It is an excellent genealogy-only site to list your new Web pages.

Richard Says:

These types of lists are kept by software manufacturers (such as Netscape), some search engines, and by almost anyone who wants to create one.

Once you get your Web site listed in the new or cool lists, you will see a large increase in visitors while you are on the list. It is definitely worth your time to get on as many of the specialized lists that you can.

Mail Lists and News Groups

Do not forget to mention your new Web pages on the mail lists you normally read, especially if you have a surname or geographic Web page that corresponds to a particular list. One mail list you definitely want to post a message to is the **NEW-GEN-URL-L@rootsweb.com** on the Rootsweb server. Another place is the newsgroup located at **comp.infosystems.www.announce.** This group is monitored by many of the people who maintain Web site lists (such as Yahoo!). It is an excellent way to advertise your site.

Still another way to advertize your new Web site is to monitor the various genealogy-related newsgroups. You can respond to queries from others asking for information. It is considered bad taste to post an unsolicited advertisement about your Web site to the newsgroup, but mentioning it when you respond to queries is acceptable.

Advanced Topics

Appendix A

This book was not intended to be an advanced book on Web page design and creation; however, this section will cover a little about some advanced topics. If you have an interest in developing your Web site with more of these advanced features, you should consider purchasing a book that covers the topic or feature you wish to learn more about.

CGI Scripts

Common Gateway Interface, or CGI, is a programming language used to run programs on a Web (HTTP) server. These external programs are known as "gateways" because they create an interface between an external source of information (the visitor's Web browser software) and the server.

CGI scripts are typically used to add the following types of features to your Web pages:

✓ Guest Books

✓ Web Counters

✓ E-mail Forms

✓ Imagemaps

✓ Other Features That Require User Input

There are two methods available to use CGI scripts. The first is to install the script on your Web space provider's computer. The second is to use a service that has CGI scripts on their server, which they allow others to access from their own Web site.

Installed on your server:

CGI scripts (programs) need to be installed on your Web space provider's server. If you do not have access to your Web space provider's cgi-bin directory, you cannot use this method of CGI scripts on your Web pages.

Generally, you cannot write your own CGI scripts if you have a free Web space account. Many of the free Web space providers will give you access to some standard scripts, however. These are usually counters, imagemaps, and sometimes other functions. You should ask your provider what CGI features are available.

Run from another server:

Simply put in the codes for the scripts you wish to use and have them reference the server where the CGI script is located. One free CGI script provider is the CGI Free Web site at **http://www.cgi-free.com/**. They offer free CGI script hosting for Webmasters that do not have access to a cgi-bin from their Web space provider. They currently offer eight scripts on their server.

If you would like to learn more about CGI, you can go to a tutorial at **http://hoohoo.ncsa.uiuc.edu/cgi/**. If you have access to the CGI directory and want to use some pre-made CGI scripts, there are a many Web sites that offer free CGI scripts. Some of these are listed on the following page.

Matt's CGI Script Site:
http://www.worldwidemart.com/scripts/

This Web site has many CGI scripts available for you to use.

Webmaster Tools - CGI Scripts:
http://www.tila.com/scripts.shtml

CGI Scripts on the Web. This is a list of various CGI-Script providers that are available on the Web.

CGI Free:
http://www.cgi-free.com/

Offers free CGI script hosting for Web masters that do not have access to the cgi-bin directory on their Web space providers server. They offer eight scripts that can be used for free on their server.

Frames

The Frames feature allows unique page designs that include such things as interactive displays of data and/or images. You have probably seen Web pages made up with frames. Usually, they are used for navigation buttons or menus. They do not disappear as you view different Web pages on their site, but are always visible (generally on the left side of the screen, Figure 169 is an example of a Web page using frames (this site is located at **http://www.nehgs.org/**).

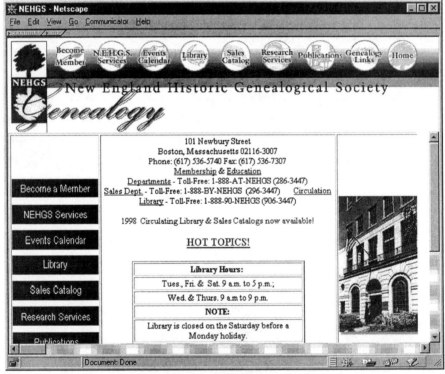

Figure 169: NEHGS - Web page showing frames

The frames feature allows you to split your Web page into multiple, independently scrolling panels, with separate documents in each panel. On a framed Web site, hyperlinks in one frame can be programmed to update the content of the other frame. Frames can make a visually pleasing navigation interface for your Web site. However, not all Web browsers are "frames-capable." As with any advanced feature, you will be limiting the number of people who can view your Web pages.

There are many uses for frames. Here are just a few:

* Keep footers and/or headers visible at all times. These may include a toolbar for selecting linked pages.

* Fixed, or scrolling, vertical lists in a left or right frame that display the selection (the hypertext link) in an adjacent frame, while keeping the list visible.

* Horizontally scrolling lists.

For more information on frames, these online tutorials can teach you:

Sharky's Netscape Frames Tutorial:
http://www.newbie.net/sharky/frames/intro.htm

Jay's guide to Frames:
http://www.columbia.edu/~jll32/html/frame.html

Netscape's Frames Tutorial:
http://home.netscape.com/assist/net_sites/frames.html

Forms

Forms are very popular. You can ask the visitor to fill out a form on your Web page then submit it. The results of the data can be sent to you via e-mail. This is a good way for you to receive feedback from those who visit your Web pages. You can also use forms to create a guest book. The best part about forms is that they won't slow the loading process of your Web page.

Figure 170 is an example of a very simple form. You can make your forms as simple or complex as you wish. If you decide to add a form to your Web page, there are several tutorials available. Following are just a few:

WebCom Forms Tutorial:
> http://www.webcom.com/html/tutor/forms/start.shtml

Idocs Guide to HTML:
> http://www.idocs.com/tags/forms/forms.html

Web Diner Forms Tutorial:
> http://www.webdiner.com/annexe/forms/wdform1.htm

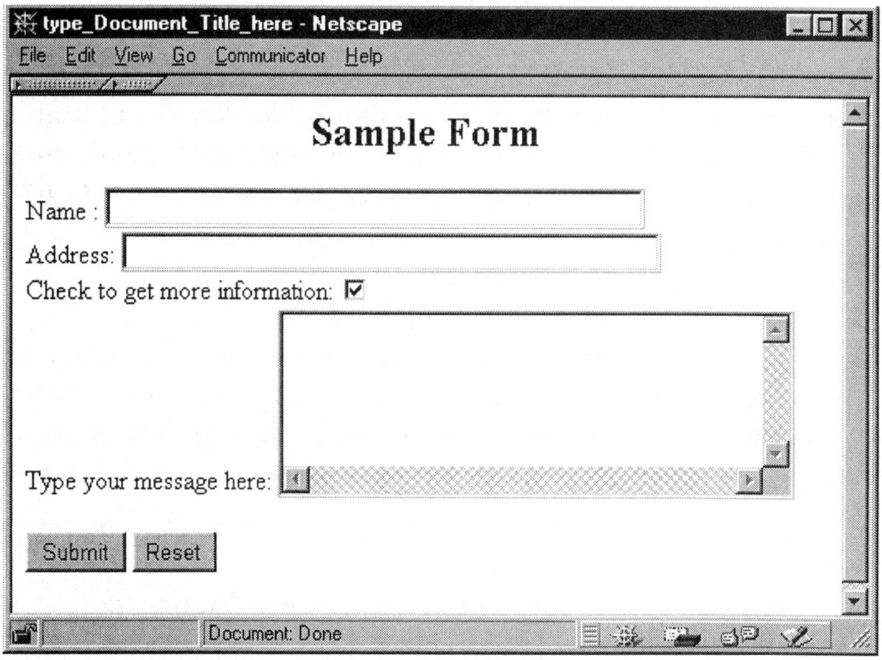

Figure 170: Sample Form

Imagemaps

Imagemaps are hyperlinks in the form of a graphic image. When you move your cursor over the graphic, the arrow becomes a pointing finger (indicating there is a hyperlink). Different areas on the image will take you to different links. This is the reason it is called an imagemap. Different areas on the image are "mapped" to various URLs. Figure 171 is a good example of an imagemap (this site is located at **http://www.usgenweb.org/statelinks.html**).

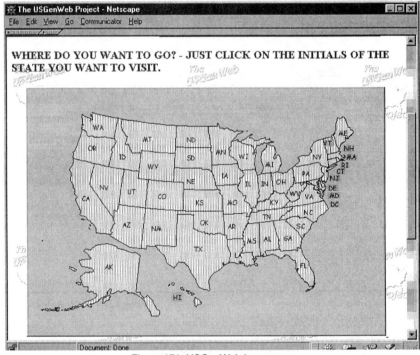

Figure 171: USGenWeb imagemap

Here are a few online tutorials about using imagemaps:

WebCom Imagemap Tutorial:
http://www.webcom.com/html/tutor/imagemaps.shtml

Kira's Web Toolbox:
http://www.lightsphere.com/dev/ismaps/

Advanced HTML programming: Imagemaps:
http://www.intergalact.com/hp/part2/part2.html

Java Scripts

Java isn't a page description (markup) language like HTML. It is an actual programming language. Description languages specify content and placement, while programming languages describe a process for generating a result. Java is a new language based on the power of networks and the idea that the same software should run on many different kinds of computers (such as IBM personal computers, Macintosh computers, or a network computer) or even with the new technologies that are now being developed. It works on any device that supports the Java platform.

There are many online tutorials available to help you learn Java and the Java Script language. Here are just a few sites:

Sun Microsystems Java Tutorial Page:
http://java.sun.com/docs/books/tutorial/index.html

The Java Tutor:
http://www.mercury.com/java-tutor/

A list of Java Resources:
http://www.apl.jhu.edu/~hall/java/

Richard Says:

Java programs are currently being developed to make the family history on your personal Web pages interactive. I do not think it will be very long before these Java applets will be available to make the genealogy on your own Web pages "come alive."

Broderbund's Banner Blue Division is the first company to offer a genealogy application that uses Java; however, you must own the Family Tree Maker program in order to upload your data onto their Web site at **http://www.familytreemaker.com/**. Also, this application will only work on their site. The Java application is called "InterneTree" and is offered, along with free Web space, for anyone who wants to publish their genealogy on the Family Tree Maker site.

The InterneTree is a form of a report file generated by the Family Tree Maker program. For an example of how to create this report, see the "Family Tree Maker" section of *Chapter 4*, on page 77.

As mentioned before, this advanced feature will only work with a Web browser that is Java-enabled. Because the browser must download the entire file in order to display it, the viewer's computer must have enough memory and storage space. If you have a large file, the viewer must also have a fast Internet connection to download the file without having to wait too long.

You can see a demonstration tree at Gary Hoffman's Web site located at **http://www.familytreemaker.com/users/h/o/f/Gary-B-Hoffman/**. When the Web page loads, click on the InterneTree in the Reports section.

Some of the Basics

Basic DOS Commands

Although this book isn't meant to teach you the DOS operating system or DOS commands, this section has been included to teach you a few of the basic DOS commands you may need to use for genealogy.

All computers must have an operating system to work. One of the first operating systems for personal computers was DOS. It has been around since 1980, when IBM introduced their first personal computer (PC). Today, most computers have a version of Windows on them.

Richard
Says:

If you have Windows 95/98, most DOS commands can be accomplished with the Explorer program. There is no need to start a DOS prompt to perform these commands (see your Windows manual for more information on the Windows Explorer program).

Here are some of the DOS commands that a genealogist would find the most useful. There are many more commands available. Check your DOS manual for more information.

CD (Change directory) Displays the name of the current directory or changes the directory.

> *Syntax:*   CD [drive:][path]
>
> *Usage:*   To change to a Webpage sub directory from the root directory, type CD\WEBPAGE
>
>   To change down one directory level, type CD..
>
>   To go back to the root directory, type CD\

COPY   Copies one or more files to another location.

Syntax: COPY [/A][/B]source

Switches: /A indicates the file is an ASCII file
                            /B indicates the file is a binary type
                            /V verifies that new files are written correctly

Usage   If you are in the C drive and wish to copy all
                            the files in the DATA subdirectory to the A
                            drive, you would type: COPY C:\DATA*.* A:

                            (The asterisk (*) is a wild card and can take the
                            place of any letters).

                            To copy a group of files with the same
                            extension (such as Web files) to the A drive,
                            type: COPY *.HTM A:

DEL (Delete or erase) Deletes or erases files.

Syntax: DEL [drive:][path]filename [/P]
                            or ERASE [drive:][path]filename [/P]

Switches: /P prompts you for conformation before
                            deleting file(s).

Usage: To erase all files in directory, type:
                            DEL *.* (CAUTION - make sure you are in
                            the directory you want to have erased.)

                            To erase only one file called filename.ext type:
                            DEL filename.ext

DIR (Directory)   Displays a list of the files in the directory and the sub-directories. It also gives the volume name and available disk space. If you use DOS 5.0 or above, it also gives the total size of the files in the directory.

Syntax: DIR [drive:] [path] [filename] [/P] [/W] [/A]

Switches: /P pauses the listing so you can view one screen at a time
/W displays the listing in wide format
/A displays all files, including hidden and system files

Usage: To get a listing of the current directory and pause it when the screen fills, type: DIR/P
If you only want to know file names, not the date and size, you can type: DIR/W

EDIT   (DOS 5.0 and above) Starts the MS-DOS editor, which creates and changes ASCII files (such as HTML files).

Syntax: EDIT [[drive:][path]filename] [/B] [/G] [/H]

Switches: /B displays editor in black and white
/G uses the fastest screen updating for a CGA monitor
/H displays the maximum number of lines possible for the monitor you are using

Usage: To edit or create a file type:
EDIT C:\INDEX.HTM
(If the file doesn't exist, the program will create it.)

MD (Make Directory)   Creates a subdirectory off the directory you are currently in.

    Syntax: MD [drive:]path

    Usage: If you want to create a subdirectory called WEB off an existing directory called INTERNET, you would type: C:\INTERNET> MD WEB

                  If you then wanted to create a subdirectory called BU off the WEB directory, you would type: C:\INTERNET\WEB> MD BU

REN (RENAME)   Changes the name of a file or files.

    Syntax: REN [drive:][path]filename1 filename2

    Usage: To rename a file from sample.doc to test.doc, you would type:
REN sample.doc test.doc

                  To rename all files in a directory from the extension of .TXT to .HTM, you would type: REN *.txt *.htm

RD (Remove Directory)   Removes a subdirectory from another directory. The directory being removed must be empty.

    Syntax: RD [drive:]path

    Usage: To remove the directory called BU from the C:\INTERNET\WEB directory, you would type:
C:\INTERNET\WEB> RD bu

VER (Version)   Displays MS-DOS version number.

    Syntax   VER

    Usage: Type VER from the C: prompt and it
                                     will display: MS-DOS version 6.22
                                     (or whichever version you are using)

Creating a Shortcut in Windows 95/98

It is important to understand how to create shortcuts with the Windows 95/98 operating system. Many of the programs in this book do not automatically create icons on your desktop so they are easy to start. This section will cover creating shortcuts on the main desktop. For more information on shortcuts, see your Windows 95/98 manual.

To create a shortcut:

*   click your right mouse button while over the desktop.

*   select "Shortcut" from the "New" menu (see Figure 172).

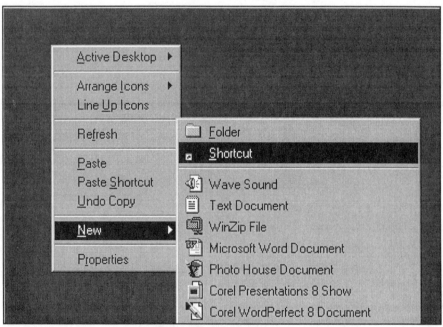

Figure 172: Pull-down menus

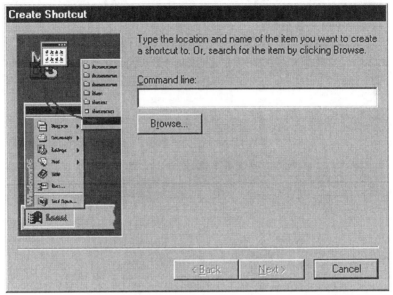

Figure 173: Create Shortcut

- Once you select "Shortcut," you will see the "Create Shortcut" screen (see Figure 173).

- Type in the name and location of the program, or you can select the "Browse" button to locate the folder and name of the program. If you select the "Browse" button, the screen in Figure 174 will then open.

- Once you have located your program with the "Browse" screen, you select the "Open" button. This will return you to the "Create Shortcut" screen, where you select the "Next >" button.

- Give the shortcut a name (such as GED Clean). Finally, select the "Finish" button and the icon will be created on the desktop (see Figure 175).

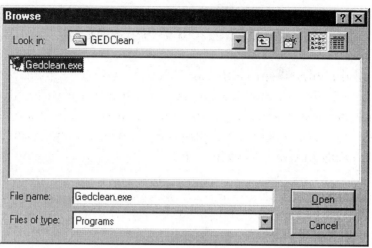

Figure 174: Browse screen

Figure 175: Icon on desktop

If it is a DOS program, you may also wish to right-click on the new icon and select "Properties." This will give you the opportunity to set many of the other features that are available for running DOS programs. For more information, see your Windows 95/98 manual.

Compression Programs

Many of the software programs and files that you download from the Internet are in a compressed format. The reason for this is that the files transfer faster when they are smaller in size. There are several different types of compression programs. The most common are zip files for DOS and Windows files, and Stuffit files for Macintosh files.

In order to use these shareware and freeware programs, you will need a compression program installed on your hard drive. Two places you can download compression programs are:

Windows:
http://tucows.lvdi.net/comp95.html

Macintosh:
http://tucows.lvdi.net/mac/compmac.html

Following is a discussion of the commonly used compression programs for DOS, Windows and Macintosh.

PKZip (for DOS)

This DOS file compression program has been around for a long time. The current version is 2.04g. It comes as a self-extracting file (named *pkz204g.exe*) which contains many different files.

To use this program, place it in a sub-directory or folder and type "pkz204g" then press <ENTER>. It will un-compress itself into about sixteen files. Once you have uncompressed it, you can start using it. To find the proper syntax for using each of the parts of the program, type the name (i.e., *pkzip* or *pkunzip*) and press <ENTER>. The proper usage will be displayed (see Figure 176). To compress a file (or files), use *pkzip.exe*. If you need to un-compress a file, use *pkunzip.exe*.

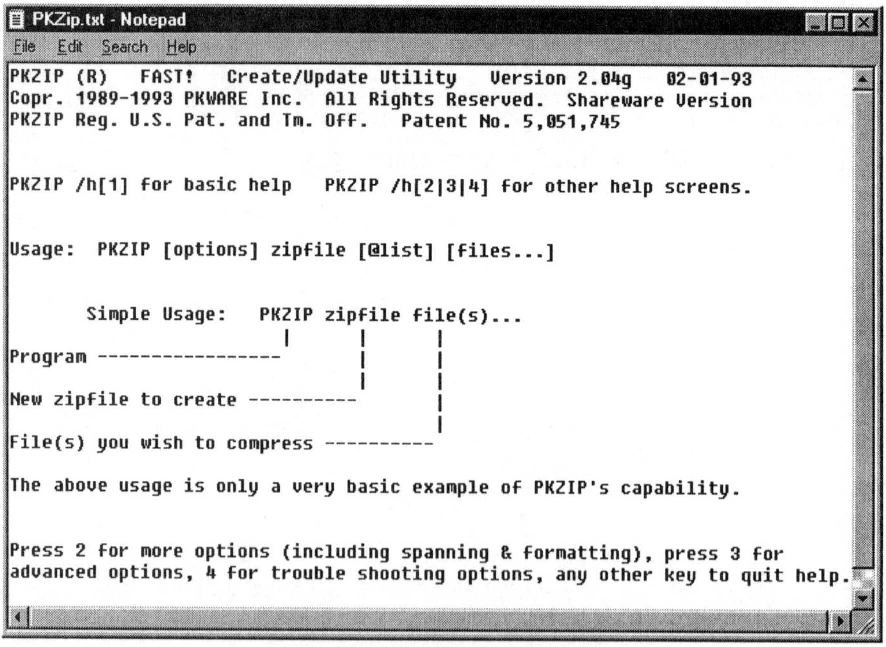


```
PKZIP (R)   FAST!   Create/Update Utility   Version 2.04g   02-01-93
Copr. 1989-1993 PKWARE Inc.  All Rights Reserved.  Shareware Version
PKZIP Reg. U.S. Pat. and Tm. Off.   Patent No. 5,051,745


PKZIP /h[1] for basic help   PKZIP /h[2|3|4] for other help screens.


Usage:  PKZIP [options] zipfile [@list] [files...]


       Simple Usage:   PKZIP zipfile file(s)...
                         |       |       |
Program -----------------        |       |
                                 |       |
New zipfile to create ----------         |
                                         |
File(s) you wish to compress ----------

The above usage is only a very basic example of PKZIP's capability.


Press 2 for more options (including spanning & formatting), press 3 for
advanced options, 4 for trouble shooting options, any other key to quit help.
```

Figure 176: PKZip - correct usage

WinZip for Windows

To install the WinZip program, you double-click on the file you downloaded. It will then start the installation program and install itself on your computer. After it is installed, it will set up icons for you to start using the program. If you are using Windows 95/98, it will also set up the program so it can be easily accessed when you are in Windows Explorer.

To use WinZip from the Explorer program, you simply place the cursor over the file you want to compress or un-compress and click the right mouse button. A pull-down menu, like the one in Figure 177, will appear. Select "Extract to." The "Extract" screen will appear (see Figure 179).

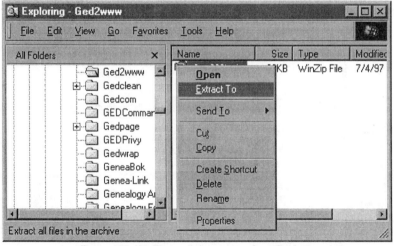

Figure 177: WinZip - pull-down menu from Explorer

You can also start the program from the icon that was created for it. The first thing you will see is the main screen (see Figure 178). If you choose the "Extract" (unzip) button, the "Extract" screen will appear (see Figure 179).

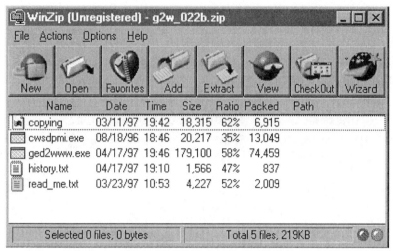
Figure 178: WinZip - main screen

From the "Extract" screen, select the location where you want to save the file or files. If you want to place them in a new folder (or directory), you select the "New Folder" button and type in the name of the new folder it will create.

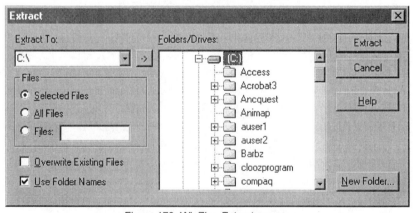
Figure 179: WinZip - Extract screen

To compress (zip) files, place the cursor over the file you want to compress and click the right mouse button. Select "Add to Zip" from the menu that pops up (see Figure 180). The "Add" screen shown in Figure 181 will appear.

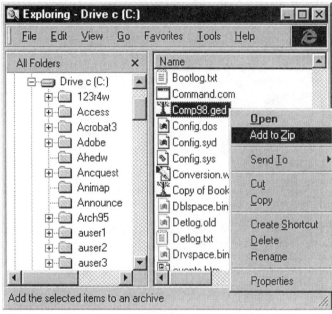

Figure 180: Winzip - Add to Zip

From the "Add" screen, you can add files to a new or existing zip file (the New and Open buttons in the "Add To Archive:" section). You can also change the compression type. Next to the field under "Compression," click on the arrow and choose the compression type from the pull-down menu. Once you have selected or created the zip file, you select the "OK" button to add the file.

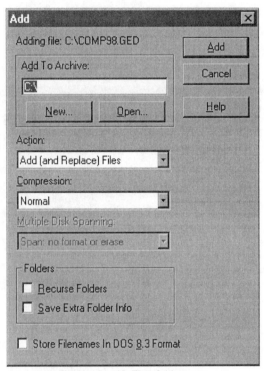

Figure 181: WinZip - Add screen

Stuffit for Macintosh

You can download Stuffit Expander or Stuffit Lite for the Macintosh Macintosh at **http://www.aladdinsys.com/products/index.html**.

To use StuffIt for Macintosh, you simply drag and drop a file from any folder onto the StuffIt icon and expand the file. You can also start the Stuffit program and choose "Expand" from the "File" menu.

StuffIt Lite features capabilities such as the ability to password protect archives, create self-extracting archives, and segment archives for fitting large files across multiple floppy disks. StuffIt Lite comes complete with an online guide.

Glossary

404 error: HTTP/1.0 404 Object Not Found. This is a common error message you get on the Internet. It indicates that the file you want does not exist on that server. You may have typed the URL wrong, the Internet may be very busy, or the file may have been deleted or moved (a change of URL address or location is a very common occurrence on the Internet).

absolute links: Hypertext links that contain the full URL of a Web page, graphic, or other link.

ActiveX: Microsoft's product which competes with Java.

address: The location of a Web site, e-mail box, or ISP. See also URL.

America Online: A commercial bulletin board service that also provides Internet access and Web page storage space to its customers.

animate: Give the illusion of movement in a graphic by showing a series of still images, each one slightly different from the previous image and the following image.

AOL: See America OnLine.

applet: A special software program, created with Java, to create special effects (such as scrolling messages) on your Web pages.

application: A program, or group of programs, typically designed for computer users.

ASCII: American Standard Code for Information Interchange (pronounced Asś-Kee). Gives a standard code number to the alphabet, numbers, punctuation symbols, and computer control codes.

attribute: Special HTML keywords that tell Web browsers how to display text on a Web page.

baud: The speed at which your modem sends or receives information.

beta: Usually used to refer to a program that has not yet been completely tested.

binary file: A non-text file. Examples would be graphic (*.GIF* or *.JPG*) or sound (*.WAV* or *.AU*) files.

BMP: Bit-mapped graphics format. This is the standard graphic format for Windows. This type of graphic file **cannot** be used on Web pages. Web pages can only handle GIF, JPG or PNG graphic file formats.

bookmark: The method of saving the URL of a Web site you may want to visit again. Called "Favorite Places" in AOL or "Favorites" in Microsoft's Internet Explorer.

bps: Bits per second. It is the speed rating for any modem that is used to connect your computer to your phone line. The minimum speed that many ISP's allow to connect to the Internet is 14,400 bps (14.4 Kbps). Most modems currently being sold are rated at 33,600 bps (33.6 Kbps) or higher.

browser: A program specifically designed to give you access to the multimedia information that exists on the Internet. Such software allows you to view documents that contain text, sound, graphics, and video. A browser also allows you to "jump" from one location to another by clicking on hypertext links. (See hypertext links).

carriage return: A paragraph mark in HTML code indicated by the <P> and </P> tags.

case sensitive: Indicates that the text entered must be in the exact case (i.e., "Web" would not be the same as "web"). Web site addresses must be typed with the proper case on certain Internet computers (those running the Unix operating system).

CGI: Common Gateway Interface. A programming language used to make Web pages interactive.

chevrons: These are used to identify/separate the HTML tags from the rest of the text on a Web page. All HTML tags are surrounded by these two symbols (< >). They are on your keyboard above the comma and period keys.

CIS: See CompuServe.

compound tag: An HTML tag that consists of more than one part.

compress: See compression.

compression: A method of reducing file size so it can be transmitted over the phone lines quicker. Some compression programs include: PKZip, WinZip, and Stuffit.

CompuServe: A commercial bulletin board service that also provides Internet access and Web storage space.

connection: When two computers are communicating with each other. Commonly used to refer to "going online."

cookies: A small file written on your hard drive that tells Web sites where you have been or specific information about you. They are written by a few of the Web sites you will visit.

counter: A system that keeps track of how many people have visited or accessed a Web page. Each access is referred to as a "hit."

cyberspace: Any of the information that is available through computer networks, including the Internet.

directory path: The final part of a URL, after the domain name and before the Web page file name. In the example **http://www.compuology.com/cagenweb/index.html** "cagenweb" is the directory that contains the file *index.html.*

distributed applet: An applet you can use without adding to your Web pages. It is accessed remotely.

DNS entry: Domain Name Server entry. The URL address typed in computers (servers) that are directly connected to the Internet. They automatically translate the URLs you type (such as **www.compuology.com**) into their correct numerical designations. This is good because it is easier for us to remember **www.compuology.com** than the corresponding IP address—which is **205.214.171.151.**

domain name: An exclusive name that identifies an Internet site. Domain names have two or more parts separated by periods (called dots). One computer may host more than one domain name, but a specific domain name points to one and only one computer.

Domain Name Server: See DNS Entry.

download: The process of copying a file from a computer on the Internet to your own computer.

dynamic: Used to describe a Web page that changes when a person visits the page, usually made possible with JavaScript or CGI Scripts.

e-mail: Electronic mail. You have an electronic "address" where you receive your e-mail, and you send e-mail to people at their electronic "address."

entire page: All the parts of one Web page (including text, graphics scripts, etc.). Several different files are needed to make up one entire Web page.

entire script: This consists of all of the information between the opening and closing chevrons (< >) on an HTML document. This would also include the HTML tags.

error messages: A message that indicates an error has occurred while accessing the Internet or loading a Web page.

event: An action generated by a user interacting with a Web page. For example, when you move your cursor over a hyperlink, it turns into the shape of a hand.

execute: To perform an action such as start a program or type in a command).

fade-in: When a sound byte (file) is begun, the sound gradually increases in volume and does not start abruptly.

fade-out: When a sound byte (file) is ended, the sound gradually decreases in volume and does not come to an abrupt stop.

fair use: Information that is in the public domain and is not copyrighted.

FAQ: Frequently Asked Questions. A list of questions and answers about a site or service.

Favorite: Internet Explorer's term for a URL that has been book-marked. (See also bookmark)

file: Information stored on a computer.

file compression: See Compression.

file transfer: See FTP.

Firewall: A security system designed to prevent unauthorized access to or from a private network (i.e., prevent unauthorized Internet users from accessing private networks connected to the Internet).

form: An area on a Web page used for input from users, generally in the form of boxes.

frame: 1 - A feature in HTML that allows unique page designs that include such things as interactive displays of data and/or images. Usually, they are used for navigation buttons or menus.

2 - An individual image in a series of animations (one picture after another with each changing slightly to give the effect of motion).

freeware: Software that is available for use without any fee.

FTP: File Transfer Protocol. A program, as well as a set of procedures or rules, for transferring files from one computer to another via the Internet.

GED: The three letter extension for a GEDCOM file (*.ged*).

GEDCOM: GEnealogical Data COMmunications. It is the method used to transfer genealogical data from one software program to another without having to re-enter the data.

GENDEX: A site on the Internet that contains an index of genealogy Web pages. Many GEDCOM-to-HTML conversion programs will create a file that can be used to register the names in your genealogy Web pages with the GENDEX server.

GIF: Graphic Interchange Format (pronounced Jiff, like the peanut butter choosey mothers choose). It is a graphic format used on the Internet.

guest book: A specially formatted Web page where people enter messages to the owner of the Web site. They can also view messages other people have left at that site.

hit counter: A program that is used to count the number of times a Web page is visited.

hits: The number of times a Web page is loaded (viewed) by a Web Browser. Some sites try to figure out how popular they are by counting the number of hits they get. See also Counter.

home page: This is the first page of a Web site. This is also the first page that loads when you type just the URL of a site. Usually it is given the name of *index.html*.

host: This refers to the computer (server) where a set of Web pages are located (stored).

hostname: The name of a computer on the Internet. For example, **byu.edu** is the host name for a computer system at Brigham Young University.

hot link: See Hypertext Links.

HTML: Hyper Text Markup Language. The language used to write Web pages. It includes text or graphical links that send you to other pages on the World Wide Web.

HTML editors: A program specifically designed to add HTML codes to a standard text document.

HTTP: HyperText Transport Protocol. Tells the computer which protocol to use in order to look at a document, picture, or site on the Internet.

hung: When a Web page or image stops loading. When this happens, you must exit that program and restart your Web browser software, or even re-start your computer. Also, what horse thieves got <g>.

hyperlink: See Hypertext links.

hypertext: A document that contains hypertext links.

hypertext links: This refers to a highlighted and underlined section of text, or a graphic, that takes you to another area of the Internet with the "click" of a mouse button.

icon: A small picture you click on to go somewhere, do something, or start a program.

IE: See Internet Explorer.

imagemap: A picture that has areas on it mapped (hyperlinked) to various URLs. A person can point to different areas of the image to jump to different Web pages.

information superhighway: Term used to refer to the Internet or the World Wide Web portion of the Internet.

input form: An area on a Web page used to allow input from users, usually in the form of boxes.

Internet: The term "internet" was originally used to describe any network that connected two or more computer networks to each other. Today, when people talk about "the Internet," they are referring to the Internet that spans the globe, connecting individuals, businesses, universities, governments, countries, and continents. The World Wide Web is only a small part of the Internet.

Internet Explorer: Microsoft's Web browser.

InterNIC: Internet Network Information Center. InterNIC describes itself as "a cooperative activity between the National Science Foundation, Network Solutions, Inc. and AT&T." They register domain names and allocate IP numbers (see IP).

IP: Internet Protocol. A numerical Internet address consisting of four sets of numbers separated by dots. (See also DNS Entry.)

ISO: International Organization for Standardization. ISO is not an acronym. The name is derived from the Greek word "iso," which means equal. Founded in 1946, ISO is an international organization composed of national standards bodies from over 75 countries.

ISP: Internet Service Provider. A company you use to connect to the Internet.

JAVA: A programming language that allows developers to create applets to be included on Web pages. These programs will be executed when the Web page is loaded by a Web browser that supports Java.

JavaScript: A programming language that was created by Sun Microsystems. This language can be added to your Web pages and will be executed when the Web page is loaded by a Web browser that supports JavaScript.

JavaScript-savy browser: A Web browser that understands the JavaScript programming language. It will know how to handle the scripts that are included on Web pages.

Java-savy browser: A Web browser that understands what Java applets are and what to do when it finds them.

JPG: Joint Photographic Experts Group (pronounced jay-peg and also known as JPEG). Is a graphic format used on the Net that stores images in compressed format.

Kb: Thousands of bits.

kbps: Thousands of bits per second. This is the common speed rating for any modem that is used to connect your computer to the Internet.

Keyword search: To perform a search of a database using specific words.

Legacy Software: A year 2000 term for older software programs. Not to be confused with the Legacy Family Tree software included in this book.

Line Break: An HTML code indicated by <BR>. This code indicates where a new line should begin (just like a carriage return in a word processor).

Line Noise: Telephone line static that interferes with data (Internet) transmissions.

Link: An electronic connection between two sites on the Net (such as the connection between you and your ISP).

Links: See Hypertext Links.

Linked: Items on the Web (text or images) that will take you to other forms of information when you point at them and click a mouse button. (See also hypertext links).

local storage: Files saved on the hard disk of your personal computer.

Lynx: An older, text-based Web browser for the Internet. It is rarely seen or used today.

markup: Modifying a plain text file by applying codes for special formatting that are read by a Web browser.

markup language: A formal set of procedures and rules for getting text ready to be presented on the Web. HTML is the most commonly seen markup language.

meta tag: A special HTML tag that provides information about a Web page. Meta tags are not visible on a Web page, nor do they affect how the page is displayed. They provide information such as who created the page, what the Web page is about, and which keywords best represent the page's content. Most search engines use this information when building their indexes.

MIME: Multipurpose Internet Mail Extensions. This is the specification used for formatting non-ASCII messages so that they can be sent over the Internet. Many e-mail software programs now support MIME.

Mosaic: One of the original browsers created for the World Wide Web. It is rarely seen or used today.

MPEG: Moving Picture Experts Group, a working group of ISO. The term also refers to the family of digital video compression standards and file formats developed by this group. MPEG files can be decoded (uncompressed and viewed) by special hardware or software.

multimedia: Web document files containing data in different formats, such as graphics, sounds and video.

Net: See Internet.

Netiquette: The etiquette for typing messages on the Internet.

network: Computers connected together.

node: Another name for a host computer.

output: The file or files created by a software program, such as a GEDCOM file.

page: See Web Page.

palette: Colors used to display an picture in graphic format. Normally made up of either 16 or 256 colors.

paragraph break: The HTML codes <P> and </P>. Used to create a separate paragraph (a blank line will be added after the text).

password: A secret code you need to logon to a computer. You need a user ID (login name) and a password for access to your ISP. You also need them for FTP access.

path: Full description of where a file is located on your computer.

PDF: Portable Document Format. A method that makes documents on the Web look the same when viewed on any computer or printed on any printer. To read, view, or print a file saved in this format, you will need a special software program called Adobe Acrobat Reader, available for free at **http://www.adobe.com/acrobat/**.

pipe character: See separator character.

PKZIP: A file compression program. It creates a file that ends in the extension *.zip* and can contain one or more compressed files. The receiver must use a program like PKUNZIP to restore the transferred files to their original state.

plain text: Text without any special formatting attributes (such as bold or italics).

plug-in: A file (or program) that adds to the capabilities or features of another program, usually a Web browser. An example would be the RealAudio plug in for Netscape or Internet Explorer.

PNG: Portable Network Graphics. This is a new graphic format for the Internet. It compresses graphics without any image loss. This graphic format is not commonly used and not many programs currently support it.

pre-formatted information: The HTML tags <PRE> and </PRE>. These codes are used to keep text in its existing layout on a Web page.

pre-release: An early version of a software program that is still in development. Such software versions will still have bugs (glitches) that must be fixed before it is released as a commercial program to the general public.

Prodigy: A commercial bulletin board service.

protocol: A set of rules on how computers will act when "talking" to each other. Protocols allow different types of computers with different operating systems to communicate with each other.

read-only access: A type of FTP access that allows you to retrieve files from a server on the Web, but not upload files to that server.

RealAudio: A commercial software program that uses streaming audio (see Streaming Audio).

reference: The use of HTML codes to tell a Web browser exactly where files are located so it can find them more quickly.

relative links: Links that contain only the Web page name, graphic name, or other filename. They do not contain the full URL address.

required attribute: HTML attributes you must include with a tag in order for the Web browser to understand what to do with it.

RIN: Record Identification Number. A number assigned by the computer to keep track of people entered into a genealogy database.

script: A text file containing commands that a Web browser will follow (as in Java Script).

search engines: A tool for looking up sites and information on the Internet. You use them to search by keywords, phrases, or topics. You can also browse through a table of contents of Web sites which that search engine has indexed. Each search engine operates a little differently, and some are better at specific types of searches than others.

Self extracting: A file created with a compression program, such as PKZip or WinZip, that un-compresses itself when executed.

separator character: A character used to separate the various values used in an applet. Normally a pipe (|) symbol is used, but the separator could also be a colon, semicolon, comma or space.

server: A computer with a permanent connection to the Internet. Other computers can connect to it. A server may contain Web pages, mail lists, or newsgroups.

service provider: See ISP

shareware: Computer programs that you can try before you buy. Often available for downloading from the Internet.

shouting: SHOUTING IS WHEN YOU TYPE IN ALL CAPITAL LETTERS IN ONLINE COMMUNICATIONS. This is considered bad netiquette.

sound files: A sound that has been recorded and saved in a computer file. A few file extensions for sound files are *.wav, .mid, .rmi,* and *.ram.*

SMTP: Simple Mail Transfer Protocol. The protocol used to send e-mail messages from one server to another.

streaming: The process of a video or audio file that executes as it is being downloaded from the Web, rather than having to download the whole file first.

Stuffit: A file compression program that was created for the Macintosh computer. Stuffit files usually end with the extension *.SIT.* It is also available for the Windows operating system.

surf: Browsing the Internet by clicking on highlighted or underlined text or graphics which activate a hypertext link, thus connecting you to a different Web location.

tags: Words and/or symbols that make up the HTML language used to create Web pages on the Internet (such as <HTML> and </HTML>).

TCP/IP: Transmission Control Protocol/Internet Protocol. The communications standard that allows different types of computers to communicate with each other. TCP/IP is the foundation upon which the Internet was built.

Telnet: In the beginning, you connected to another computer on the Internet by way of a program called Telnet. You typed in commands on a command line, and Telnet located the other computer and established a connection with it. All communication via Telnet was and still is text-based.

text editor: A program that allows you to change the contents of a text file. DOS uses the *Edit* program; Windows 95/98 uses the *Notepad* program; and Macintosh uses the *SimpleText* application.

text file: A file in ASCII format, usually ending in the extension *.txt*.

TIF: Tagged Image File Format. This is a popular graphic file format. It **cannot** be used on Internet Web pages.

transfer mode: Determines how the files on your computer are broken down to be sent over the Internet and re-assembled on the Web server.

transparency: A technique that allows a single color, usually in a GIF image, to be set as transparent, or see-through.

uncompress: To expand a file that has previously been compressed by a compression program.

Unix: The computer operating system that has served as a foundation for much of the programming of the Internet. Often found on very large, main-frame computers.

unzip: To expand a file that has previously been compressed by a compression program (see PKZip and WinZip).

upload: Transfer your files to someone else's computer, such as a computer on the Internet.

URL: Uniform Resource Locator. The electronic address of a document, or Web page, on the Internet. It functions like a "street address," indicating where the document or file is located. These addresses look something like this: **http://www.compuology.com/**.

user ID: The name you choose when you sign up with an ISP. You need this name and a corresponding password to logon to the system.

utility: A program that performs a useful function, such as the PKZip compression program. Utility programs can often provide useful features that were left out of major programs.

video files: Files that contain video clips. Some common extensions for video files are *.avi*, *.mpeg*, *.mpg*, and *.mov*.

Visual Basic Script: An easy-to-use programming language developed by Microsoft.

W3C: See **World Wide Web Consortium**

WAIS: Wide Area Information Service. A powerful tool used to search for information in libraries and databases on the Internet.

WAV Files: Sound files used on the Internet. They end with the extension *.wav.*

weaving: The process of installing and configuring an applet or JavaScript into a Web page.

Web browser: See Browser.

Web editor: See HTML editor.

Web graphics: Images used on a Web page (see also JPG, GIF and PNG).

Web page: A multimedia document (HTML document) on the Web. They generally end in the extension *.htm* or *.html.* Although considered a single Web page, when viewed it may be many screens long.

Web site: A location (server computer) that contains many Web pages.

Webmaster: The person responsible for maintaining a Web site.

weight: The combined size of each file or material that is transferred from the Web to a browser in order to be viewed. A general rule is to keep Web pages less than 250K in weight.

WinZip: A Windows or Windows 95/98 file compression program. See also PKZIP.

wired: Being connected to the Internet.

World Wide Web: Also known as the "The Web." A system that can handle multimedia functions over the Internet. It is made up of two parts: browser software that can "read" or "view" multimedia documents, and server computers that can support and maintain multimedia documents. The Internet and the World Wide Web are not separate entities. The computers that store Web pages are part of the Internet network.

World Wide Web Consortium: Founded in 1994, the W3C was set up to develop common protocols for the evolution of the World Wide Web. They are an international industry consortium, jointly hosted by the Massachusetts Institute of Technology Laboratory for Computer Science [MIT/LCS] in the U.S.; the Institut National de Recherche en Informatique et en Automatique [INRIA] in France; and the Keio University Shonan Fujisawa Campus in Japan.

WWW: See World Wide Web.

WYSIWYG: What You See Is What You Get. This indicates that the way a document is displayed on your computer screen is the way it will look when it is uploaded to the Web or printed.

zip: See zip file.

zip file: A file that has been compressed with either the PKZIP or WinZip programs. This makes the file smaller so it takes less time to send over the Internet.

Bibliography

Arends, Marthe. *Genealogy Software Guide*. Genealogical Publishing Company, 1998.

Homer, Alex and Ullman, Chris. *Instant IE4 Dynamic HTML*. Wrox Press Ltd., 1997.

Renick, Barbara and Wilson, Richard S. *The Internet for Genealogists: A Beginner's Guide, Fourth Edition*. Compuology, 1998.

Stauffer, Todd. *Using HTML 3.2, Second Edition*. Que Corporation, 1996.

Walsh, Aaron E. *Java for Dummies*. IDG Books Worldwide, Inc., 1996.

Index